Spiritual Theology

DATE DUE

DATE DUE

DEMCO, INC. 38-2931

SPIRITUAL THEOLOGY

The Theology of Yesterday
for Spiritual Help Today

Diogenes Allen

COWLEY PUBLICATIONS
Cambridge
Massachusetts

Published in the United States of America by Cowley Publications, a division of the Society of St. John the Evangelist. No portion of this book may be reproduced, stored in or introduced into a retrieval system, or transmitted, in any form or by any means—including photocopying—without the prior written permission of Cowley Publications, except in the case of brief quotations embodied in critical articles and reviews.

Library of Congress Cataloging-in-Publication Data:
Allen, Diogenes.
    Spiritual theology: the theology of yesterday for spiritual help today
    / Diogenes Allen.
        p.   cm.
    Includes bibliographical references and index.
    ISBN 1-56101-130-4 (alk. paper)
    1. Spirituality—Catholic Church. 2. Spiritual formation—Catholic
    Church. I. Title.
    BX2350.65.A44   1997
    248—dc21   97 -623
                                                                    CIP

Permission is gratefully acknowledged for use of material by the author previously published in *Essentials of Christian Community*, Ford and Stamps, ed. (Edinburgh: T & T Clark, 1996), "Manifestations of the Supernatural According to Simone Weil" in *Cahiers Simone Weil* (September 1994), and *Quest* (New York: Walker and Company, 1990).

Cover art: *The Angel Leads St. John to Heaven*, from the *French Apocalypse*, early fourteenth century

This book is printed on recycled, acid-free paper and was produced in the United States of America.

Fourth printing

Cowley Publications • 907 Massachusetts Avenue
Cambridge, MA 02139
800-225-1534 • www.cowley.org

Dedicated to
Timothy Gerard Allen
in recognition of his invaluable help as my research assistant

CONTENTS

Acknowledgments

This study was begun through a Pew Evangelical Scholarship for the academic year 1990-1991, and completed through a Fellowship from the Center of Theological Inquiry, where I was in residence for the academic year 1994-1995. I am also indebted to Thomas Gillespie, President of the Princeton Theological Seminary, who made it possible for me to accept these grants.

I would also like to express my gratitude to many individuals for their interest, encouragement, and help: Daniel Hardy, director of the Center of Theological Inquiry; Jean-Loup Seban, of the Chapelle Royale, Brussels; the Sisters of the Community of the Holy Spirit, St. Hilda's House, New York City and St. Cuthbert's House, Brewster, New York; Michael Buckley, S. J., and Father Robert Imbelli, both of Boston College; Thomas H. Schultz, Community of the Holy Cross (Anglican); Bill Placher and David Dawson, colleagues at the Center of Theological Inquiry, and Richard Burnett, Princeton Theological Seminary, all three of whom read chapter 9; and finally Jane M. Allen and Mary Elizabeth Allen. Of course, I bear all responsibility for whatever errors and blemishes are to be found in this study.

INTRODUCTION

A few years ago my wife was a member of the silent auction committee for a school fair. Various services were to be offered to the highest bidder, with the proceeds going to the school. One member volunteered to examine an investment portfolio, another donated one hour of legal advice, and one couple offered to act as waiter and waitress for a party. When it was my wife's turn, there was a noticeable pause, since everyone knew I was a clergyman. In a very matter of fact way, my wife said that her husband would be glad to give the highest bidder an assessment of his or her spiritual condition.

Of course, this offer was greeted with a burst of laughter; perhaps just hearing about it makes you smile. Somehow it seems absurd to mention in a normal social setting that people do have a spiritual condition, let alone that it is possible to assess it as one would an investment. Yet we do care about how we are progressing in life, although we usually assess our progress in terms of the ascent (or descent) of our career. We give far less attention to an assessment of the kind of person we are, the kind of person we can become, and the kind of person we ought to become according to God.

It is just as well that my wife's offer was not taken up, so that my inability to assess people's spiritual condition was not exposed. At that time I found myself very much at a loss concerning spiritual matters, even though I was a successful teacher of philosophy and theology to students preparing to be ministers. If anyone ought to know about such matters, I should. What troubled me at that time is not easy to put into words, even now: I found myself wondering again and again what it would be like actually to live every moment of one's life with an awareness of God.

I do not mean that I actually *wanted* to live that way, because it would be quite daunting—this constant awareness of being in God's presence. Still, I was troubled by my ignorance. In spite of my religious faith, the ability to preach sermons and to give lectures that were as good (or bad) as those of the next person, most of the time God seemed remote. Although I had a doctorate in philosophy and theology, and had read a lot of books, I did not really know what it meant to have an awareness of God in daily life, or how one went about achieving it. How was it that in all my church attendance and advanced education I had not learned such an elementary matter?

Finally, I decided to ask an older and more experienced colleague who I felt was a sympathetic sort of person with an open mind, not given to platitudes. After I explained what was troubling me, he thought for a while and then asked me how old I was. I said, "Thirty-eight." He replied, "I think what you are approaching is the age forty crisis."

I have since learned this was not the case, and my condition would have been easily recognizable by anyone familiar with spiritual theology, a branch of theology that has been neglected in recent times. My condition is called a desire for God's "habitual presence." By taking part in common religious practices such as going to church, reading the Bible, and praying before meals, sooner or later we usually feel a vague but persistent urge for something more, an urge that we cannot describe very well. Unless frustrated, this desire can occupy more and more of our attention, and lead to a hunger for God's continual presence.

In spiritual theology this condition is not merely recognized; guidance is provided on how that hunger may be satisfied. In time, a person who follows this guidance usually becomes increasingly aware of God's presence. Although most of the time the center of our attention is taken up by something else, God's Spirit is present at the edges of consciousness, enveloping us and everything else of which we are aware. This awareness of

God varies in intensity, and we can learn to increase the intensity by a simple shift of attention, just as we can glance up from a piece of work for an instant to notice something in our surroundings of which previously we were only vaguely aware. Some degree of habitual awareness is fairly common among those who allow the desire that arises out of regular religious practices to develop freely. Without some guidance, however, all too often this urge for something more does not come to its fruition in an habitual presence.

I learned all this because my quandary led me to read some classics in spiritual theology, such as Gregory of Nyssa's *Life of Moses* and Maximus the Confessor's *Four Hundred Chapters on Love*. Had I or my colleague read them earlier we probably would have recognized my condition for what it was. I suspect that what happened to me has happened and continues to happen to a lot of people who are not equipped to make spiritual assessments of themselves or to help other people understand themselves better. This lack of knowledge arises partly from the fact that academic theology has narrowed its focus and neglected the field of spiritual theology. Even when spiritual theology is read, usually it is not read with the appropriate questions in mind but is treated as strictly "devotional"—intended to warm our hearts but not to involve the mind or to be important to theological inquiry.

A widespread theological amnesia in the church means that if our hearts and minds are to be nourished and guided, we have to recover a great deal. Although writing about his own country, Yanis [John] Ritsos, a contemporary Greek poet, captures some of this need in his poem "The Graves of our Ancestors":

We have to guard our dead. Our enemies
might disinter them, steal them; then
we would be in double danger without their protection. How
can we live
without our homes, our furniture, our fields and mainly
without the ancestral graves of our fighters, our
philosophers....

Content with little, modest, silent now,
they are indifferent to votive offerings, vain glories. It
might be better
to have just a simple stone, a pot of geraniums as a secret
sign,
or nothing even. It might be safer to keep them inside us if
we can,
it might be better still not even to know where they lie.
The turn things are taking today—who knows—
we might disinter them ourselves with our own hands, one
day, and throw them away. [1]

The great spiritual theologians such as Evagrius of Pontus,
Gregory of Nyssa, and Maximus the Confessor are ignored by
most theologians and pastors. Have we utterly lost them, and
many others, because of the rise in modern times of a secular
mind that makes them appear old-fashioned? Has the progres-
sive emergence of world culture made them seem provincial?
Actually, it is not modern developments that have led us to
discard a great deal of our heritage, but church teachings themselves. It was my theological, not my secular, education that
limited me so. I was taught a great deal about the sources used
by writers of the Bible, for example—so much so that I was
afraid to rely on any verse because if I looked around, I expected
to find some scholar or other who would say that it was a later
addition, with the implication that it could not be relied upon.
Both biblical study and theology were cluttered with so many
options and so many issues that conversation in the seminary
and other academic gatherings resembled the plight of people
after the disaster of the tower of Babel rather than the deep
communion brought by the Holy Spirit at Pentecost.

I recall only too well walking home one evening through the
lovely New England countryside and being moved by the close-
ness of God. It was as if God's arms enfolded the world I was
walking in, but I reluctantly yet firmly drove the thought and
feeling away. I had been taught, as all good students of Karl Barth
were taught, that natural theology was impossible. Even to
attempt to go from nature to God was positively wrong; nature

was closed as a source of knowledge of God. It led to an idol, the God of the philosophers, whereas we were to rely solely on the supernatural revelation of God as presented in the Bible. Every stirring from nature and through nature was to be firmly resisted as a temptation. Since most of the great theologians of the past taught that the created order reflected God's wisdom and majesty, Barth's views (at least the way I understood what my teachers said) effectively dismissed both nature itself and what theologians had said about nature as a source of knowledge of God.

Although these examples are highly personal, many people, including the clergy, suffer from similar difficulties. It takes a positive effort to overcome them in order to receive the full wealth of our inheritance. We must cease to regard spiritual classics and the heart-stirring words of early theologians as merely "devotional" and not to be confused with theology or with critical thinking. Rather than being occasionally stirred by devotional literature, we can actually become aware of God's presence everywhere, whether in academic theology or in our daily life. Only then will we be free of the need to "accept" the teaching of the church with a grain of salt and endure its dead weight, rather than being inspired and guided by it.

Ironically, we find more confidence expressed in the relevance of our Christian heritage outside the institutional church than within. A growing body of literature by distinguished thinkers like George Steiner, Robert Bellah, Charles Taylor, and John Millbank shows the inadequacies of naturalism and its claims that nothing lies beyond the explanations given by the physical sciences. They all argue that naturalism cut us off from rich cultural resources, including Christian ones, for understanding ourselves and our world.

In a collection of essays entitled *Modernity on Endless Trial,* Leszek Kolakowski, the eminent Polish philosopher who was expelled from the Communist party in 1966, frequently points out that the modern world is deeply indebted to Christianity for many of its greatest achievements in ethics, politics, and the arts. Furthermore, he claims, the restraining and inspiring influence of Christian faith is needed today in order to restore the balance between two competitive tendencies in western culture: the tendency to make claims to final and ultimate truth, and a critical attitude that so undermines all claims to truth that it tends toward skepticism, relativism, and nihilism. Kolakowski points out that intellectuals can analyze the desperate condition of western intellectual culture as it loses confidence in itself, and they can even show the value and need of the Christian religion. But what is needed, he claims, is faith: "to spread faith, faith is needed and not intellectual assertion of the social utility of faith." [2]

All too often Christians are hampered and frustrated in their faith by a lack of knowledge. Many of them are thoughtful people, but they do not have enough information; it is as though they have only a few pieces of a jigsaw puzzle and are trying to put them together to form some sort of recognizable picture. Sometimes churches provide enough pieces to make some sort of picture, however crude and limited, so that people can respond with love to what they see. They might even find that the Christian picture gives some guidance and insight into the deep things of life. Their hearts are in the right place; they have responded to the goodness that Christianity seeks to portray, and through prayer they interact with God even though they cannot think about God coherently. But it is vital to recover our heritage in a useable form so that people who are attracted to Christianity can gain greater understanding. We must show that the old is not obsolete and ideas that may be new to many are not inconceivable. Instead, they shed light on our world and nourish our lives.

Notes
1. Yanis Ritsos, *Gestures and Other Poems*, Nikos Strangos, trans. (London: Cape Golliard Press, 1971), 28.
2. Leszek Kolakowski, *Modernity on Endless Trial* (Chicago: Chicago University Press, 1990), 9.

CHAPTER ONE

WHAT IS SPIRITUAL THEOLOGY?

N ot long ago I heard a short story read aloud. Virtually every word of the story seemed to grip the audience and afterwards I wondered why. It was not simply because it was a good story that had been read with great artistry; rather, the audience heard it unfold without knowing which part of the story would be important. For someone to come out of a house, get into a car, and slowly drive away is a prosaic event. But when this action is part of a story it can, as it did, hold our attention because it just might turn out to be significant.

In a well-constructed short story everything makes a contribution to the overall effect, just as every detail in a great painting is important. But we do not experience everything in our actual lives this way: only some of our life is interesting. As our life unfolds, most of it is utterly prosaic. Well-constructed stories appeal to us because all the events make a contribution to the whole. Perhaps we wish that all the events in our lives were as interesting or at least contributed to some overall meaning.

The Christian life is like a story. Life has a goal and there are various paths leading to that goal which make all of life significant. However, when too much stress is placed upon the beginning of the story—the experience of Christian conversion—it may appear to us that with conversion we have already reached our goal. I have written this book on spiritual theology in part to answer the questions, "What is there for us to do after conversion? What about people who are born into the faith and do not have a conversion experience they can point to?"

Leo Tolstoy, the great nineteenth-century novelist and religious writer, had a very powerful conversion experience. He assumed, however, that with his conversion he had reached the final stage of the spiritual journey. As a matter of fact, a simple glance at the field of spiritual theology makes it obvious that he was at the bare beginning of the Christian journey. From the very beginning it has been taught that, with God's help, conversion is followed by the effort to overcome the damage done to our human nature by sin and by our own previous behavior and attitudes. We are to begin the long process of learning to control the destructive tendencies of our personality. We can hope for transformation because, with our conversion, our lives become centered on God—with God's help we hope to achieve what we cannot achieve by ourselves.

Tolstoy failed to focus enough of his attention on the need to deal with his deeply flawed personality. The emotional relief and joy of his conversion was so great that he thought he could move from conversion to the love of neighbor in one giant step. That is why, in spite of his newfound faith, Tolstoy continued to be grossly inconsiderate of other people, especially his wife and children. Oblivious to his own considerable faults, he became a self-professed pundit on proper Christian behavior and wrote scathing attacks on the Russian Orthodox Church for what he saw as its perversion of the gospel. Precisely because he was a greatly gifted person, not only his virtues but also his vices were on a grand scale. Tolstoy failed to take sufficient account of the tenacious power of human sinfulness, which must be taken seriously before we can begin to love our neighbor with the kind of love that Jesus exemplified in his teachings and life. Conversion and the goal of loving our neighbor are separated by a vast distance that can only gradually be closed with considerable effort and help.

An important division within spiritual theology, called *ascetical theology*, is devoted to giving us guidance on how we may progressively reduce the size of this gap. Our conversion, which first turns us toward God, is not the terminus but merely the first stage of the Christian life. If we are to obey Jesus' commandment to love our neighbor as ourself, we have a great deal to do in the interval between our conversion and our death. Our conversion leaves us with much to do; it actually sets before us the task of coming to terms with our deep inadequacies so that we may love our neighbor better and come to love God with all our heart, mind, soul, and strength.[1]

Many Christians are uneasy with the idea that we are to make an effort to overcome our inadequacies because it sounds like "works righteousness," as if our salvation depended on something we do rather than wholly on God's grace. But we must remember that God is as fully active and present in our lives when we are making an effort as when we are not. In both instances we rely wholly on God for our existence and powers. It also helps us to remember the distinction between justification and sanctification. As the great Protestant reformer John Calvin put it, justification and sanctification are twins. They are both the work of Christ, but each is a *distinct* work. Justification is our forgiveness or pardon by God apart from the law because of Christ's death on the cross; sanctification is the process by which we actually begin to become holy, free of the effects of evil and full of charity or divine love. Justification is the *beginning* of sanctification. Both require divine grace. Divine grace does not mean that there is nothing left for us to do. Quite the contrary, it is precisely because of divine grace that we are able to begin to seek freedom from the effects of sin and evil, and to begin to love in the way Christ loves.

Because our life is more than an interlude between our conversion and our death, the entire task of spiritual theology is to guide us in our attempt to obey the two great commandments that summarize the entire Jewish Law: love of God and love of neighbor. It teaches us where to focus our attention after our conversion so that we do not think we have done all we ought to do and thus neglect a vital step in the process of coming to love God and our neighbor.

∴ ∷

So far I have mentioned only some of the main steps in the spiritual life. Even though the entire journey is not the same for everyone, it will be useful at this point to give a sketch of the dominant pattern of the spiritual life that was taught in the early centuries of the Christian church. This pattern developed from prolonged study of the Bible and from extensive practical experience. Although it was taught by many very influential theologians and teachers, they did not demand rigid conformity, so aware were they of the freedom of God's Spirit. Even in those cases in which all the main steps were followed, they were not always followed in every detail or with the same emphasis on every step of the journey. Nonetheless, this early pattern of the Christian life influenced other distinctive spiritual traditions as they arose over the centuries, and it continues to influence them today.

There are three stages in the journey, which is often called the threefold way. The first stage is *praktike*, or practice. *Praktike* consists of three steps:

(1) repentance or conversion;

(2) the development of virtue or human excellence, which includes the redirection of the emotions or passions; and

(3) love of neighbor.

This first stage is usually called the "active life" and is what we mean by *ascetical theology*. It contains a great deal of practical advice on how to overcome our evil actions, thoughts, and dispositions so that as our flawed human nature is increasingly restored and renewed we become more free to love our neighbor as ourselves. Evagrius of Pontus, whose writings were the fountainhead of ascetical theology and who died at the end of the fourth century, held that in the active life we exhibit in our lives the victory of Christ over evil, sin, and the devil, and we praise God with the beauty of our lives.

The contemplative life, or *theoretike,* has two parts that together make up the second and third stages of the threefold way: the indirect and the direct love of God. The second stage, the indirect contemplation of God, is called *physike*. From it we get our word "physics." In ancient Greek, however, *physike* meant "nature." In spiritual theology *physike* refers to the entire created universe of nature, human beings, and invisible spiritual beings. In contrast to the first stage of the threefold way, in which we are actively engaged in shaping our disordered lives around God's commandments, the second stage is focused on contemplation, in which we are receptive rather than active.

In the past this distinction between the active and contemplative life was often symbolized by the story of two sisters, Mary and Martha, from Luke's gospel (10:38-42). Mary, embodying the contemplative way, sits at Jesus' feet; Martha, symbolizing the active way, prepares a meal. Leah and Rachel, Jacob's wives, were also used to symbolize the active and contemplative life. In the Roman Catholic Church the active life has traditionally referred to members of religious orders who are engaged in teaching, preaching, or social work, while the contemplative life has meant prayer and religious seclusion. But the early church—and the Eastern Orthodox churches to this day—treated Mary and Martha, Leah and Rachel, as symbols of two tendencies within one person's life rather than as symbols for different kinds of lives. In other words, all Christians are to practice both aspects of the spiritual life to the degree suitable to their temperament and occupation. This is much more in tune with the Protestant reformers, who hotly rejected the practice of monastic vocations and the contemplative life as the Christian ideal, insisting that all socially useful occupations were fully *spiritual* vocations. Even though the reformers greatly emphasized the active life of repentance, virtue, and service to our neighbors, they also stressed the importance of Bible study and prayer for all Christians, not only for contemplatives.

In the second stage of the threefold way—*physike*—we focus upon the indirect contemplation of God. Through regular and not episodic contemplation of the world about us, we are increasingly able to experience all creation (including our own life) as a gift, and to discern God's presence in the entire created universe. The philosopher and mystic Simone Weil is particularly articulate about indirect contemplation of God through the beauty of the universe as a whole, despite our vulnerability to illnesses and accidents.[2] Kallistos Ware, a bishop of the Greek Orthodox Church, refers to nature as "God's book," a very common expression from the earliest centuries:

> It is to see God in all things and all things in God—to discern, in and through each created reality, the divine presence that is within it and at the same time beyond it. It is to treat each thing as a sacrament, to view the whole of nature as God's book.[3]

Because of the ecological crisis, people today have a new awareness of the environment. One reason God may seem remote to many Christians is the loss of our ability to receive God's presence through the created universe. Were we open to God, God would be always present to us, because whether we are in church or not, we are always surrounded by the natural world. We would be able to experience the truth of the words from a Greek poem that St. Paul uses to express the nearness of God: "He is not far from each one of us. For 'In him we live and move and have our being'" (Acts:17:27b-28). Such an awareness would give the ecology movement a powerful rationale in addition to our legitimate fear of despoiling the whole of creation. One of my major aims in this book is to enable us to learn how to "read" the book of nature as a companion to the book of scripture.

As our human nature begins to be transformed, it will yield to us a more intimate knowledge of God than the physical universe can because human beings, in contrast to the rest of creation, are made in God's image. Because of our kinship to God, we long for fellowship with God as well. According to the mystical theology of Gregory of Nyssa, as our fellowship with God increases, we desire more and more to will the will of God. To be like God is to act as God acts. Perhaps we can see more of God in saintly people, but all of us mirror God to the extent to which our lives fulfill God's intentions. Since Jesus' human nature was never in need of restoration because he always lived in perfect conformity to God's intentions and because he is the divine Word incarnate, his life is "the image of the invisible God" (Col. 1:15; cf. 2 Cor. 4:4).

Our slow transformation also enables us to discern the spiritual—in contrast to the merely factual or literal—meaning of the Bible. For example, "Jerusalem" refers not only to an historical city, but also to the Christian church, the human soul, and the heavenly Jerusalem, our final home. An important aspect of contemplation has always been study and meditation on the spiritual meaning of the Bible with the intention of growing in our likeness to God through greater knowledge of God. Although the contemplative tradition offers many examples of extravagant allegorical interpretations of the Bible, the desire to seek God's purposes and make these the subject of our meditation and prayer is an essential part of the Christian life. For many people today, the historical-critical approach to the Bible has effectively cut them off from an indispensable source of knowledge about God. As we will see, adapting more traditional approaches to scripture helps bring into balance contemporary and traditional understandings of scripture.

Indirect contemplation, or *physike*, then, focuses on three things: the physical universe, human nature, and the Bible. The emphasis placed on each varies considerably from theologian to theologian and from teacher to teacher. But for all of them scripture is of vital importance.

Progress in the contemplative life brings us to the final stage of the threefold way, which is the direct contemplation of God. This third stage is sometimes called *theoria*, from which we get our word "theory," but in this context it refers to the highest kind of knowledge. The word *gnosis* was widely used to refer both to indirect and direct contemplation of God. In Latin Christianity direct knowledge of God is referred to as "infused contemplation" by Thomas Aquinas and others to signify that direct knowledge of God occurs wholly through God's initiative and not our own. Here God's presence is no longer mediated through creation, whether it be through the physical world, through other creatures, or through scripture. We no longer see God dimly in a mirror, but face-to-face (1 Cor. 13:12). In this earthly life only a very few people have this knowledge of God. They are said to have a foretaste of the joy we will enjoy eternally, and a vision of God that all Christians will enjoy after death in the kingdom of God.

In the ancient church the very word "theology" was sometimes restricted to this direct knowledge of God, and *theoria* came to be called mystical theology. This is not to be confused with the idea of mystical experience, because in Christianity mystical theology is always rooted in Christian doctrine. The God who is known is *explicitly* the triune God, Father, Son, and Holy Spirit. For example, Cyril of Alexandria, writing in the early fifth century, describes mystical union with God through the widely used image of iron heated in fire:

> To participate in the divinity of the Son...is...to be penetrated by divinity—just as the red-hot iron in the fire is penetrated by the heat of the fire—allowing the beauty of the inexpressible nature of the Trinity to shine in us.[4]

As fire causes iron to glow, so too does the Holy Spirit enable the divine life of the Trinity to show itself in our life of love.

Some of the confusion over mystical theology and mysticism derives from the "way of negation" in Christian doctrinal theology and spirituality, particularly in the influential fifth-century works of Dionysius the Areopagite, which stress momentary, ecstatic experiences of union with God in this life. I will have more to say about this later, particularly when we study the fourteenth-century *Cloud of Unknowing* and see that in this work the way of negation culminates not in ecstasy, but in more prosaic habitual presence. At this point, all we need to remember is that mystical theology is not the same as mysticism—at least as mysticism is generally understood today—because doctrine is essential to it. The term "spiritual theology" more accurately describes these teachings for us today than "mystical theology," as it includes doctrinal theology, liturgy, and individual and corporate behavior.

∾ ∾

The outline I have given here of the Christian pilgrimage needs to be expanded considerably before we can use it to make more than the crudest assessment of our own or other people's spiritual condition, and before we can use it to guide us in our own journey. Later I will flesh out the threefold way with material drawn from the entire history of the church, not just the ancient period. At this point, even with only a bare outline, I would like to ask the question, "What do most of us do to improve our spiritual health?"

We attend church. In worship the redemptive purposes of God are celebrated, and worship frequently leads to the stirring of a desire for God's habitual presence. But, as in my own case, unless we have some explicit instruction in spiritual theology, we are not likely to recognize this stirring for what it is, nor to know how to direct it. In time we may even be surprised that in worship we no longer receive the spiritual nourishment we once did.

The most common activities of church life today are revivalism, Christian education, pastoral counseling, and social action. With revivalism, being a Christian is virtually identified with a conversion experience, so not enough is done to guide people's subsequent spiritual growth. The other three common activities of church life—Christian education, pastoral counseling, and social action—try to overcome the limitations of the revivalist tradition. They also have had to fill the vacuum caused by theologians' neglect of sanctification, which is concerned with spirituality. All these activities are needed and have done a great deal of good, but they have not yet taken sufficiently into account the teaching of spiritual theology.

One of the purposes of this book is to offer help to those people who cannot find what they are looking for in academic theology as it is usually practiced today, and for whom neither church worship nor the major activities of church life provide enough explicit spiritual guidance. I do not promise that this book will actually give an assessment of your own spiritual health. A doctor must examine a patient by taking blood pressure and discussing symptoms in order to make a diagnosis and prescribe a treatment. But doctors can also talk in a general way about what people can do to promote good health and about which symptoms indicate they should consult a physician. So too the account of the "classic" Christian spiritual journey which I am going to fill out can give you an idea of where you are in the spiritual life, offer some suggestions from those who have traveled the road before you, and mention some of the hardships and dangers of the journey.

I want also to offer some help to those who would like to begin reading some of the great classics of spirituality. Many modern accounts neglect fundamental principles of spiritual theology, especially the vital connection of Christian spirituality to the Bible and Christian doctrine. To make it easier to read classics of spirituality we will integrate the account of the Christian journey with seven simple questions that can be asked of any book on spirituality, questions that will inform you of what to look for as you read. They will help you to notice differences in the accounts of a particular stage of the Christian pilgrimage by various writers. Becoming aware of the variety may be very helpful, because one account may connect with your life more fruitfully than another. By posing these questions *explicitly* we can discover the writers that help us most.

The first question we must ask is: *What is the goal of the spiritual life?* Classics of spirituality have described this goal as the vision of God, the vision of the Trinity, union with God, participation in God's life and being. For Calvin the goal was "to know God and to enjoy God forever." Since the idea of union with God, or participation in God's life and being, is unfamiliar to many Christians today, it is important to note that the familiar description of the church universal as the body of Christ rests on the conviction that Christ has united himself with us. All these ways of expressing the goal focus on the object of our attention: Christ. Other descriptions of the goal found in the classical accounts concentrate on what *we* may become—we realize the image of God within us in order to resemble God more closely, or to be more like Jesus, or more holy, or more perfect with a pure love for God. It seems that more than one way is needed to express the different aspects of the goal. A writer may emphasize one aspect more than others, or even neglect some aspects altogether.

In contrast to the ultimate goal, there are the proximate and more immediate goals, such as learning to control our emotions and love our neighbors. One of the tasks of spiritual theology is to discuss the relationship between and compatibility of these different accounts of the goal, as well as the relationship between the ultimate goal and those goals that are nearer to hand.

The second question to ask of any account of the spiritual life is: *What is the path to the goal?* I have described the threefold way as the "classic" path that developed during the early centuries of the church, but there is considerable variety among those who write of the spiritual life. This variety should not disturb us. On the contrary, it is wonderful that there is variety because people differ in intellectual interests, emotional temperament, gifts, and roles in life; we also live in different periods of history and in different kinds of societies. All of these factors affect which path or part of a path will be most relevant to us. For example, all accounts of the path stress the need for preparation and the purgation of vice. Although the lists of vices that need to be purged may overlap significantly, they are not identical because the theologians are addressing different audiences. George Herbert, a seventeenth-century poet and Anglican priest, stressed the need to purge the vices of lust, gluttony, gambling, and idleness because his account of the Christian pilgrimage was directed primarily to courtiers, and these vices were particularly prevalent at royal courts. Herbert wrote in verse for a similar reason: in his day people at the court prized poetry and wit and, as Herbert put it, "A verse may find him, who a sermon flies."

The third question we can ask is: *What motivates us to begin to the spiritual life?* Here again we find a long list: fear, remorse, or guilt, confusion or loneliness, a desire for justice, for truth, for understanding, and a sense of awe and mystery. And once again, variety is valuable because each of us begins to seek God for different reasons. A knowledge of the range of motives may enable a person to find those reasons that are uniquely helpful.

The fourth and fifth questions form a pair: *What helps us make progress in the spiritual life, and what hinders us?* Prayer, meditation on scripture, and retreats are frequently recommended as aids; lack of faith, flagrant sins, and, paradoxically, pride in our progress are commonly cited as hindrances.

The sixth question is closely related to this pair: *How do we measure progress?* That is, on what basis are we to assess our spiritual state? This is the question with which I began, but now we see that it belongs within a larger framework of questions. The Continental reformers, and their followers to this day, strongly objected to the notion of spirituality as a *process* because it smacked of works righteousness, of something we can control. Rather than speaking of progress, they preferred to speak of Christian *maturity.*

For the seventh question we must ask, *What are the fruits of the Spirit?* Among the fruits usually mentioned are love, joy, peace, friendship, discernment, and victory over death. The letters of St. Paul and St. John are particularly rich on this topic, while the classic biblical texts are Isaiah 11:2 (the seven gifts of the spirit of the LORD) and Galatians 5:22 (the fruit of the Spirit). Among theologians, one of the most comprehensive treatments of this theme is given by Bonaventure's *The Tree of Life,* based on a study of the birth, life, death, and resurrection of Christ. Jesus is described as the tree of life, in an allusion to the tree of life that was in the Garden of Eden. If we are joined to Jesus, the tree of life, our lives will bear the same kind of fruit his life bore.

These seven questions do not by any means exhaust the number of questions that may be asked of the classical texts on the spiritual life, but they can guide a beginner through the maze. In addition, these questions specify precisely what I mean in contrasting spiritual theology and doctrinal theology: each is a different field of theology because it asks different questions. Spiritual theology is the field that studies spirituality; spirituality itself is focused on the Holy Spirit, who brings to fullness in our individual lives and in the Christian community the work of

God achieved in Christ. Doctrinal theology is the work of theological investigation and is concerned with questions like the relationship between the three persons of the Trinity and the nature of their unity. A doctrinal theologian might ask, Is the Holy Spirit a person in the same sense of "person" as are the Father and the Son? She asks this because in western theology the Holy Spirit is regarded solely as the bond between the Father and the Son. In what sense is the personhood of the Holy Spirit to be understood? Some theologians speak of the Holy Spirit as the corporate identity of the Christian community, which is a different sense of personhood than that of the Father and Son.

These and other questions posed by doctrinal theology are perfectly legitimate questions, but they are different from the questions asked by spiritual theology. Both sets of questions are *theological* questions, a fact that is not widely recognized today. Yet there is no legitimate reason for limiting theology to the kinds of questions investigated by doctrinal theology, hence excluding those questions that investigate God's work in us through the Spirit. In academic theology today the practice of theological investigation is restricted to only one major branch of theology—doctrinal. Moral theology, once a clearly recognized branch, is usually treated today as Christian ethics.

The great theologians of the past used to treat both kinds of questions, those asked by doctrinal and those asked by spiritual theology. Only relatively recently have doctrinal and spiritual theology been pursued in isolation from each other; for most of the history of theology, they interacted richly. To make progress in doctrinal theology it was essential to mature in one's spiritual life, because theological understanding and spiritual progress went hand-in-hand. Although doctrine was not identical with spiritual theology, the notion of spiritual progress without increased knowledge of God or doctrinal inquiry without spiritual fruits was inconceivable. To give only one example, the longest chapter of John Calvin's *Institutes of the Christian Religion*, a recognized classic in doctrinal theology, is about prayer. Calvin's *Institutes* is seldom read today with spirituality in mind, but Calvin treats all the questions pursued in spiritual theology.

In the following chapters I will turn to the spiritual life itself and describe the Christian doctrines that guide and shape it. Then I will expand on the seven questions that largely make up the field of spiritual theology, including an elaboration of the threefold way, which is the classic treatment of the path to God.

Notes

1. See, for example, Dom Marc-François Lacan, "Conversion and Kingdom in the Synoptic Gospels," in *Conversion*, Walter E. Conn, ed. (New York: Alba House, 1978).

2. See especially Simone Weil's chapter "Forms of the Implicit Love of God," in *Waiting for God* (New York: Harper & Row, 1973).

3. Kallistos Ware, "Ways of Prayer and Contemplation," in *Christian Spirituality: Origins to the Twelfth Century*, Bernard McGinn and John Meyendorff, eds. (New York: Crossroad, 1985), 398.

4. Quoted in Vladimir Lossky, *The Vision of God* (Crestwood, N.Y.: St. Vladimir's Seminary Press, 1983), 98.

CHAPTER TWO

THE JOURNEY
AND THE GOAL

As we have said before, a well-constructed story appeals to us because everything that happens contributes to the whole, and we may sometimes wish that all the events of our lives contributed to some overall meaning in the same way. In *Orthodoxy* G. K. Chesterton describes how he eventually came to the conviction that life was like a story—an adventure story. Adventure stories usually have some important goal that requires great dedication if it is to be achieved; they tell of the valor of loyal companions who face danger and endure losses in achieving that goal. Chesterton shows that these and other features are also present in the Christian understanding of life, and he goes on to say how the Christian understanding of life gave shape and direction to his own.

Chesterton discovered for himself what today is widely called "the narrative form of human life." We quite naturally express who we are in the form of a story about ourselves. We introduce ourselves to other people by telling them where we are from, where we were educated, who we know, whether we are married and have a family, what are our goals, and so on. We do this because our identity is achieved slowly, through time, and it cannot be expressed apart from an account of our specific passage through time.

Recognizing the narrative form of human life is so important that it is the basis of the attempt by the contemporary philosopher Charles Taylor to reform the practice of contemporary philosophy. In his book *Sources of the Self: The Making of Modern Identity,* Taylor claims that western civilization, in forming our moral and spiritual identity, has given us our understanding of human life and our views of what makes life worth living. But recently a narrower understanding of what it is to be modern has cut us off from our past and so from the narrative account of our own identity. Our former way of seeing ourselves as people able to find and realize a worthwhile life is now indefensible, and as a result, present-day philosophy does not provide any basis for judging whether or not someone is living a worthwhile life.

Larger frameworks are needed in order to bolster our sense of moral awareness. Taylor claims that traditionally much of our self-understanding and moral energy has come from frameworks provided by narratives, such as the Jewish, Christian, Marxist, and liberal humanist accounts of history. To see our life as part of a larger pattern carries tremendous moral power; such narratives not only enable us to retrieve and draw upon past achievements, but also put us in contact with the sources of good in our universe and their transcendent source in God. When a story or narrative involves human growth and flourishing, it treats life as if it were a journey. A person, or group, or the race itself moves from a worse to a better condition. This understanding of life is shared by most of the great philosophers of the past, such as Plato, Aristotle, Plotinus, Descartes, Spinoza, and Hegel, as well as all the great theologians of Christianity and other religions of the world. All of them see life as a movement away from illusion, error, or sin toward enlightenment, truth, or renewal.

This view of life as a journey means that Christian spirituality should not be regarded as an esoteric, hole-in-the-corner enterprise—a sort of personal hobby. Insofar as it is concerned with a journey from a bad state to a better state, spirituality is a *human* enterprise. Everyone is on one sort of journey or another; failure to recognize this is to fail to be human and to suffer great deprivation. Walker Percy, the late novelist and metaphysician, once said in conversation, "I have learned that the most important difference between people is between those for whom life is a quest and those for whom it is not." The vision of a quest confers meaning on our lives. It enables us to see all that happens as moving us closer to or further from our goal, and to make distinctions between what helps and hinders us in our journey. There are religions other than Christianity that have inspired similar visions, but we are not in a position to decide the respective merits of one over another until we have lived and moved along one path for ourselves. Any great religion requires a profound change in us before we can truly begin to understand and practice it.

In chapter one I proposed that the first question we may ask of any account of the spiritual journey is: *What is the goal of the spiritual life?* This goal has been described in various ways—as the vision of God, the vision of the Trinity, union with God, participation in God's life and being, the pure love of God, and the condition of knowing and enjoying God forever. All spiritual writers agree that whatever this goal is, it can ultimately be reached only after death, when the kind of life we will have is very different from our present life. Does that mean that the goal lacks any real connection to our present life?

We can overcome this false impression by looking at Jesus' teachings on the two great commandments. According to the accounts in Matthew and Mark, when asked which was the greatest of the commandments, Jesus replied, "'You shall love the Lord your God with all your heart, and with all your soul, and with all your mind.'" He immediately added, "And a second is like it: 'You shall love your neighbor as yourself.'" In Matthew's gospel Jesus adds that the law and the prophets depend on these two commandments; in Mark's, he notes approvingly the remark of a scribe that to obey these commandments is more important than burnt offerings and sacrifices (Matt. 22:34-38; Mark 12:28-34). If love is lacking, the motivation for keeping all the commandments is lost. In the gospel of Luke, moreover, Jesus gives the same answer to a different question. A scribe asks him, "Teacher, what must I do to inherit eternal life?" From

Jesus' reply, we learn that we receive eternal life through obeying these two commandments (Luke 10:25-28). All of the law's prescriptions for daily life, therefore, have their basis in these two commandments, and to obey them is to follow a course of life that culminates in "eternal life." That is why this life and the life to come, in spite of their differences, are integrally connected: one leads to the other.

Jesus also taught that if we love God with all our heart, all our soul, all our strength, and all our mind, and love our neighbor as ourselves, we are able to do so only through the gift of God's gracious love. Without God's grace, we are unable to love as we are commanded to love. Love of neighbor is like love of God because in both cases the same divine love is at work in us, even though the objects of our love differ. In one case our love is for people, and in the other it is for God. Our primary relationship to other people is one of service and concern for their welfare. God is not in need, however, so our love for God is marked by having every aspect of our being—heart, soul, strength, and mind—centered on God and permeated with love for God.

"Heart" refers to our desire to find what is good or valuable so that we may possess and enjoy it, as reflected in Jesus' remark, "Where your treasure is, there your heart will be also" (Luke 12:34). Our greatest good is to belong to God as God's beloved. "Soul" is another word for life, and in this context refers to loving God in every aspect of our lives. "Strength" refers to our energy, which is to be devoted to God, and to devote all our strength to God suggests the intensity of our devotion. "Mind" refers to learning how all that we know and understand relates to God, so that we may see how all that is created, including our personal and corporate life, is related to God, so that nothing is seen or understood without our being aware of its connection to God.

The two great commandments are a standard by which we can measure our lives and a promise that through grace we will become people who love fully. The overriding aim of our lives is to obey God by loving God and our neighbor. We do not always love as we should, but we are promised that with God's Spirit at work in us we will be able to love more and more. The task of the spiritual life is to obey the two great commandments perfectly, so that our will becomes one with God's will. The union of our will and God's will fulfills Jesus' prayer: "Your will be done, on earth as it is in heaven" (Matt. 6:10).

⌣. ⌣

Now that we see that the goal of the spiritual life, though distant in its realization, is nonetheless directly connected to our present-day actions, we need to examine more closely our ultimate destination. The different descriptions of our ultimate destination I mentioned at the start of this chapter bring out different aspects of eternal life. Let us begin with a term all Christian writers use for the ultimate goal of the Christian life: the vision of God. The word "vision" indicates a *direct* knowledge of God whereby we are brought face-to-face with God, so to speak, with nothing between us. Love of neighbor and of God eventually leads us into the presence of God, whom otherwise we know only indirectly through what God creates, directs, and reveals. Through the perfection of love and our resurrection from the dead, we finally are in a condition to be fully present to God and for God to be fully present to us.

The phrase "vision of God" (or "beatific vision," as it is frequently put) implies that we are in the presence of the supreme good. Since God is the source of all goodness, surpassing all the created goods we desire and admire, to be in direct, intimate contact with God is to be in a state of delight. Origen, a third-century theologian whose writings were a wellspring of eastern and western Christian spirituality and exegesis, saw the erotic love of man and woman described in the Song of Songs as an allegory of Christ's love for the church, and our love for God. Other theologians, such as Bernard of Clairvaux, did not hesitate to use human erotic love as an analogue for the delights of God's unveiled presence. For these writers, something that is a created good—human sexuality—is used to indicate an unlimited good—the presence of God—that we do not fully enjoy but are able to describe through comparisons.

Human erotic love in its tenderness, its concern for another, and its sense that the beloved is irreplaceable also suggests that knowledge of God is communion with God. We will find our fulfillment by being able to share more and more in the infinite good that God gives us in love, and to which we respond with a pure, joyful love. In our union with God, while still remaining creatures, we participate in the divine life of love found in the Trinity. Abba Isaac, whose teachings have come to us by way of John Cassian, speaks of the union of the believer with Father and Son:

> And this will come to pass when God shall be all our love, and every desire and wish and effort, every thought of ours, and all our life and words and breath, and that unity which already exists between the Father and the Son, and the Son and the Father, has been shed abroad in our hearts and minds, so that as He loves us with a pure and unfeigned and indissoluble love, so we also may be joined to Him by a lasting and inseparable affection.[1]

This is a more personal and less forbidding way to express the notion of union with God than the term "deification," which has been used in the eastern church since the second century.

God begins to share his life with us now through the gift of his Spirit. Without violating our will or nature, God's Spirit helps us increasingly to understand and imitate God so that we come to resemble God. This is why many spiritual writers describe the goal of the Christian life in terms of *becoming*—becoming perfect, holy, and Christlike. We become like what we know. As Origen wrote, "The whole reasoning mind, [as it becomes] purified of the filth of vice, washed of all stain of malice, will feel, understand and think as God."[2] To become perfect is to be assimilated by God. Knowledge of God is thus inseparable from love, since to be perfect as God is perfect is to love as God loves (Matt. 5:43-48).

The conviction that we come to resemble what we know is similar to the ancient Greek philosophical principle that only like knows like. But there are vital and unbridgeable differences between these two ideas. In ancient Greek philosophy it is a necessary condition of knowledge that we are like what we know, and the very fact that we know something shows that we have an affinity with it. This is why, in Plato, knowledge of the eternal Forms implies that our souls too are immortal. Unlike material things, these Forms do not come to be and then pass away; the part of us that knows them must be like them and so is able to survive bodily death.

In Christianity, however, it is the knowledge of God that produces likeness to God. We are created in God's image and likeness, but we have lost the capacity to obey and know God properly. In Plato it is our bodily appetites that keep us from knowing ultimate reality; for Christians it is sin, guilt, and death. We do not have the ability to overcome these barriers, but what enables us to know God and through that knowledge become like God is based on God's action, especially the act of becoming incarnate. Our entire life is drawn into the life of God by the presence of God the Holy Spirit who comes to us through our baptism into the death and resurrection of Jesus. As John the Baptist said of Jesus, "I have baptized you with water; but he will baptize you with the Holy Spirit" (Mark 1:8).

Knowledge of God is not a conceptual grasp of truths, but a response to God's creation, incarnation, and crucifixion. In each action, God makes a sacrifice. In order to create God must pull back, so to speak, and give up being the only reality. For God to become incarnate is for God to become degraded, to move from a greater to a lesser order of being. For God to be crucified is for God incarnate to endure the consequences of sin and evil to such a degree that the Son felt abandoned by the Father. To respond to such a reality is to be moved to repentance and to become one who cares for others in the same manner as God does, for "whoever says, 'I am in the light,' while hating a brother or sister, is still in the darkness" (1 John 2:9). If our actions do not resemble God's actions, we do not know God; we only come to know God by acting as God acts.

Augustine of Hippo taught that God has made us this way so that we may draw near to him:

See how God will have us approach him, making us first like him that we may approach him. "Be as your Father which is in heaven, who maketh his sun to rise on the evil and on the good, and sendeth rain on the just and on the unjust." As charity grows in you, working upon you and recalling you to the likeness of God, it extends even to enemies....The measure of your growth in charity is the measure of your approach to the likeness; and in that measure you begin to be conscious of God.[3]

Through God's Spirit at work in us, we are able to begin to love.

Love of neighbor, which is the goal of the active life, allows us an indirect knowledge of God here and now: in loving our neighbor, we resemble God. Thus the first stage of the threefold way, which has as its goal love of neighbor, and the second stage, which is the indirect knowledge of God, are both connected to our ultimate goal. Love connects our life here and now with our life hereafter.

We must be cautious, however, in describing the ultimate goal of the spiritual life because our knowledge of God is so limited. Perhaps we should simply say: "Our ultimate goal is heaven, but we cannot say very much about what heaven is like. It surpasses all the joys we now know and it lasts forever," and leave it at that. But we cannot, because some people seem to have experienced more. In Christian theology and spirituality some people, such as St. Paul, claim to have had in this life a foretaste of heaven. They have actually experienced God's presence face-to-face and known the joy of that presence. According to the third stage of the threefold way, exemplified in the fifth-century mystical writings of the pseudonymous Dionysius the Areopagite, God chooses to give some people a momentary and ecstatic awareness of the divine. What are we to make of this?

Many of the great Protestant theologians of the twentieth century—Barth, Bultmann, Brunner, Ebeling—were hostile to the very idea of Christian mysticism. For them mysticism was an essentially pagan element that has survived in Roman Catholicism and in the eastern churches, and their distrust of it extends to exalted religious feelings of the kind found in revival-ism and pietism. In his monumental study *The Vision of God,* theologian Kenneth Kirk has put his finger on the problem that such theologians have with the idea of ecstatic experience.[4] Even though the vision of God is the ultimate goal of the Christian life, and even though it is possible to have ecstatic experiences that anticipate the life to come, it is a mistake to think that the primary *purpose* of the spiritual life is these moments of ecstatic religious experience. Such ecstatic union with God in this life is solely at the disposal of God. Unlike the other division of the spiritual pilgrimage, it is a special and specific vocation that is granted only to a few. It could hardly be the primary purpose of life to seek what cannot be sought, or to seek what is intended only for a few.

It is clear from all spiritual writers that the knowledge of God that occurs in an ecstatic state is knowledge received through love, not through the intellect. All that can be known of our final goal is what love can comprehend of God. What love can know is all we may experience of the world to come. But the primary purpose of our lives in *this* world cannot be ecstatic experience of union with God, for this implies the neglect of all our other faculties, including our senses and our minds, for the love of God.

Finally, there are other views of what it means to know God "face-to-face." For example, for the author of the fourteenth-century mystical treatise called *The Cloud of Unknowing* a foretaste of heaven is not momentary ecstasy, but instead the more prosaic experience of God's "habitual presence." This is particularly telling since the *Cloud* author believes himself spe-cifically called to know God face-to-face. As a translator of Dionysius's *Mystical Theology* into middle English, this author is aware of the way of negation. Yet unlike in Dionysius, the way of negation does not culminate in ecstasy, but in an experience of God's presence in which we remain aware of ourselves and are normal in every way. The *Cloud* author not only describes meeting God face-to-face in the "dark cloud of unknowing" as an experience of habitual presence, but he also adds:

There are those who think that this matter of contemplation is so difficult and frightening that it cannot be accomplished without a great deal of very hard work beforehand, and that it only happens occasionally, and then only in a period of ecstasy. Let me answer these people as well as I can. There are some who by grace are so sensitive spiritually and so at home with God in this grace of contemplation that they may have it when they like and under normal spiritual working conditions, whether they are sitting, walking, standing, kneeling. And at these times they are in full control of their faculties, both physical and spiritual, and can use them if they wish, admittedly not without some difficulty, yet without great difficulty.

This experience of God's habitual presence not only is an alternative to ecstasy, but is superior to it. Those who know God face-to-face in a rare, momentary ecstasy may eventually progress, by God's grace, to know God continually, or "habitually":

For if and when God pleases, it may well be that those who achieve it at first but seldom, and only with great effort, shall afterwards have it when they will and as often as they like.[5]

According to both Dionysius and the *Cloud* author, in the way of negation all positive statements about God are to be rejected, thus leading us into a cloud of darkness. This is not to be confused with nihilism, for the darkness is caused by the overloading of our senses and minds when we are met by the divine reality, just as a bright light can blind us. As a line of a well-known Welsh hymn puts it, "'Tis only the splendor of light hideth thee." Yet the God whose presence causes the darkness, and who is experienced as love, is the same God who created the universe and became incarnate in Jesus Christ. The darkness we enter is the *other side* of what is known. It is not an unqualified darkness of unknowing, but the other side of what can be spoken of, imaged, and conceived.

Even though very few people have an experience of God face-to-face, their experience is a witness to the primacy divine love is to have in our lives. Furthermore, the fact that we cannot perceive God with our senses or conceive of God with our minds reminds us that God is a mystery. Nonetheless, it is good to remember that any of us can experience or be emotionally affected by God's presence as it is revealed to us through nature, through other people, and through scripture. Even though the doctrines of Christianity always have precedence over personal experience, the heart has an important place in Christian spirituality. Late nineteenth-century Protestant theology rejected the hallowing of subjective religious experience by pietist and revivalistic movements, but these abuses do not warrant the rejection of all affectivity in Christian spirituality. Experiences of the heart are for many people a way to God, as in this passage from the diary of Frank Hedrick Allen, a Rhodes Scholar, which was written almost ten years before his death from cancer at the age of thirty-three.

> We climbed to the peak above Windermeer, between Windermeer and Ulswater, today. Such a moment of wind and the elements and incredible beauty I've never had before. I have had similar moments. Points at which, if they were to continue, I've felt as if I would have a moment of insight and clarity which would make all other things simple and understandable. A moment of real poetry. I'm never able to stay where I am long enough, it seems, to have that long-awaited moment of insight. I have had the thought twice in the last two days, once above Windermeer and once at Glen Nevis, that dying at such moments would not be a loss, or rather that such a moment or an experience was worth dying for.[6]

This passage also echoes Simone Weil's view that the beauty of the world can calm the restless ego and give us the feeling that something of great importance is about to be given to us. Weil points out that the world never does yield what it promises, as if the world through its beauty pointed toward the truth that lies beyond the world. In her own case, it was a powerful experience of Christ's presence that triggered the intense philosophical study and prayer that led her to connect her experiences to her understanding of herself, God, and the world. But it is the nourishment given by God in various ways, including the beauty of the world and experiences of the presence of Christ, that sustains people like Frank Allen and Simone Weil in their trials.

⌣ ↝

The final question we need to consider in examining the goal of the spiritual life is the idea of Christian perfection—what it means to be perfect as God is perfect. The Christian understanding of contemplation has to be freed from Platonic and Aristotelian assumptions that the goal of life is the contemplation of a static and never-changing reality. This is an extremely large and difficult topic in both philosophy and Christian theology, but for us the question is this: do our lives, which are to resemble God's life, attain perfection when they cease to change? Superficially, at least, the use of expressions such as "eternal rest" for heaven certainly suggests that this is the case.

Gregory of Nyssa, one of the great Cappadocian theologians of the fourth century, is very explicit on this question. In his *Life of Moses* and *On Perfection*, perfection means a neverending increase in goodness and excellence, not stasis. Gregory loves to use Paul's image of the Christian life as that of a runner exerting himself to the fullest extent for the glorious prize that awaits—knowing God face-to-face. Since God is infinite and shares his infinite life with us fully, we never cease to grow in excellence and goodness throughout our life in God's presence. Gregory therefore tells those who lament because human nature is changeable that change is not only toward what is evil, but also toward what is good:

> Let no one be grieved if he sees in his nature a penchant for change. Changing in everything for the better, let him exchange "glory for glory" [2 Cor. 3:18], becoming greater through daily increase, ever perfecting himself....For this is

truly perfection: never to stop growing towards what is better and never placing any limit on perfection.[7]

Gregory is not only considered one of the greatest theologians of all time, he is also widely said to be the orthodox theologian most influenced by Platonism. Theologians today often attack the ancient Greek philosophers and the theologians of the early church because they view God's perfection as "static." Gregory, however, rejoices in growth and understands the goal of the Christian life as one of neverending growth and change, which is the meaning of perfection. As one of the greatest expositors and defenders of the Nicene settlement, which affirmed the full divinity of the Word of God incarnate and the Holy Spirit, Gregory saw God the Holy Trinity as a neverending, dynamic life of giving and receiving. That is the nature of God's perfection. Gregory of Nyssa thus enriches our understanding of neverending joy, since contemplation is not merely looking at God but the continuing development and growth of our own person as we interact with the source of all that is good and desirable.

If we are uncomfortable with this notion of a life in which the goal is never fully reached, perhaps some analogies will help. A scholar who enjoys her work knows that however hard and long she works, there will never be an end to her research. There is simply too much to know, while new interpretations and new data continually arise. This fact does not make her enjoy increasing her knowledge any less. There is also more great music than any one of us could hear in a long lifetime even if we did nothing but listen to music. More music is being composed all the time. This does not cause us to give up listening to music, nor does it destroy the enjoyment of listening.

The great value of the second stage of the threefold way is its emphasis on the mind rather than on the evocation of emotional states. The mind, properly used, aids our transformation as we move closer to God. It also reminds us that the Christian does not only seek to master all of the passions that hinder our love of neighbor, but desires to obey the first of the two great commandments, which is to love God with all our hearts.

To live a life that resembles God's life requires us to relearn a long-neglected characteristic of God the Trinity: namely, diversity in unity. In the eastern church it is taught that all of us share the same nature, which is Christ's, and so all are united in Christ. But each of us is different as well, reflecting God's diversity in unity—one nature but in three persons. This means that human beings, thanks to their unity in Christ, may be obedient to God through lives that are quite diverse. It is not a desert father, a contemplative in a cloister, a religious taking a vow of poverty, or a priest or minister who is the paradigm of the truly Christian life. All of these are admirable and legitimate Christian vocations, but as the Protestant reformers emphasized, our likeness to Christ lies above all in service to others. This service is offered through work that produces goods and services in society.

Less well-known but also persuasive on this point is Francis de Sales, the great seventeenth-century Roman Catholic bishop of Geneva, founder of the Order of Visitation, and author of *Introduction to the Devout Life*. He protested with energy against the common view of his day that perfection was impossible outside the cloister. Unlike his contemporaries who wrote on the spiritual life only for men and women who had withdrawn from the world, he wrote for those who led outwardly ordinary lives:

> It is an error, or rather a heresy, to wish to banish the devout life from the regiment of soldiers, the mechanic's shop, the court of princes, or the home of married people.... Devotion must be exercised in different ways by the gentleman, the worker, the servant, the prince, the widow, the young girl, and the married woman. Not only is this true, but the practice of devotion must also be adapted to the strength, activities, and duties of each particular person.[8]

Such an affirmation of ordinary life and work was a religiously liberating and life-enhancing discovery at that time, but we need to go much further today. Since the time of the Reformation and Renaissance we have seen significant growth in our understanding of what is possible and desirable for human life. Our awareness has deepened of what makes earthly life worthwhile, what things are worth doing, admiring, and achieving. With increasing personal freedom in many parts of the world, it has been possible for people to discover the rich potential in human nature. In the seventeenth century Francis Bacon, the greatest proponent of the value of the new science, stressed that science was part of our regeneration and restoration, an expression of our love of neighbor, and a way to obey God. The way for Bacon had been paved by the theologian Hugh of St. Victor in the twelfth century, for whom preparation for heaven did not mean neglect of the earth or living a minimal earthly existence. Of course, there are temptations of pride, avarice, and competitiveness, but the Christian way is also riddled with temptations—above all the failure to obey Christ by neglecting to develop our talents. No single life, even that of God incarnate, can contain and be all that is worth doing and being in God's sight.

Nineteenth-century romanticism, for all its sentimental excess and the pursuit of feelings for their own sake, nonetheless opened our eyes to the value of human emotions as a register of the greatness of human life. They can degenerate into self-preoccupation and self-indulgence, but they can also give us someone like Kierkegaard, whose turbulent wresting with the rich variety of human life has opened our eyes to the presence of God the Holy Spirit in vast expanses of human activity. I recall a clergyman once telling me after a wonderful concert that for the first time in his life he realized that by enjoying the beauty of the music he was *obeying* God, while before that experience obedience had always been associated with unpleasant tasks for him. We are still learning how many more possibilities there are for living a Christian life. Any way that we can improve and enrich human life is living the Christian life, and every way in which we enjoy and appreciate what is good and beautiful can be an act of obedience.

Notes

1. John Cassian, *Conferences,* in *Nicene and Post-Nicene Fathers,* 2nd series, Philip Schaff and Henry Wace, eds. (Grand Rapids: Eerdmans, 1955), 11: 404.

2. Quoted in Vladimir Lossky, *The Vision of God* (Crestwood, N.Y.: St. Vladimir's Seminary Press, 1983), 48.

3. Quoted in John Burnaby, *Amor Dei: A Study of the Religion of St. Augustine* (London: Hodder & Stoughton, 1938), 81-82.

4. Kenneth Kirk, *The Vision of God* (London: Longmans, Green, 1931), x.

5. *The Cloud of Unknowing,* Clifton Wolters, trans. (New York: Penguin Books, 1978), 146-148.

6. *American Oxonian* (Spring 1988), 75: 2, 178.

7. *On Perfection,* in *St. Gregory of Nyssa: Ascetical Works,* Virginia Callahan, trans. *The Fathers of the Church* (Washington, D.C.: Catholic University Press, 1967), 58: 121-122.

8. Francis de Sales, *Introduction to the Devout Life,* John K. Ryan, trans. (New York: Doubleday, 1989), 44.

CHAPTER THREE

CONVERSION

In the last chapter we considered the first of the seven major questions of the spiritual life, *What is the goal of the spiritual life?* Now we are ready to turn to the second: *What is the path to the goal?* With this question we start our examination of ascetical theology, which is the first stage of the threefold way and is entered into by conversion.

The idea of conversion as the entrance to the path we are to follow is perfectly familiar to most of us. Conversion literally means to turn around and face in another direction; in relation to the Christian life, it simply means to turn from the path we have been following and take another. Because of the powerful revivalist tradition in American religion, however, conversion in most people's minds has come to mean a "born-again" experience. For many, their understanding of conversion is based on television evangelists, and for some, this popular idea of religion is a barrier to becoming a Christian. This is especially true for well-educated people once they are convinced that religion is merely a matter of the emotions and so is not to be taken seriously by a thinking person. Those who have had a born-again experience, on the other hand, may think that to become a "real" Christian it is necessary to have a unique, life-changing experience.

Such conversion experiences do occur, but we need to consider more than just these experiences in order to understand the nature of conversion. Lamin Sanneh, a professor of missions at Yale University, recently pointed out in a lecture that in Africa about six million people a year become Christians, four million by birth and two million by conversion. Conversion is not understood primarily as an individual rite of passage, but as a corporate one—the act of joining others who seek to move toward a new social order. An individual who converts is turning from one way of life to enter into a new order that is being created, one based on God in Christ. Conversion is thus the transformation of an entire cultural order, each individual participating in the overall transformation. Sanneh also noted that this understanding of conversion is much closer to that of the early church. Often when the New Testament relates that a householder converted to Christianity, such as the baptisms of Lydia and of Paul and Silas's jailer in Philippi, it adds that the entire family and their slaves followed suit (Acts 16: 15, 31-34).

Of course, stories of intense experiences of a personal conversion do exist in the Christian scriptures, notably in the case of Saul's experience on the road to Damascus and Philip's conversion of the Ethiopian eunuch. A personal experience, however, no matter how intense, is not the essence of conversion or even necessary to it. People who have had a dramatic conversion experience and describe themselves as "born again" Christians sometimes assume that to be a full-fledged Christian everyone must have a similar experience. Others, who consider themselves to be Christians but who have not had a dramatic conversion experience, question this assumption. These two different understandings become a source of contention in many churches. If both parties could agree that in Christianity the crucial thing is to be devoted to God, much friction could be avoided.

To gain a better understanding of what conversion means, we need to understand what we are to turn from and what we are to turn toward. The redirection of a person's life in conversion may be extremely sudden, so that he or she is very much aware of the change, or so gradual that it is almost imperceptible, even though a gradual change can result in a complete redirection. For example, if we were to stand still and hold one of our arms out vertically, in twelve hours it would be pointed in the opposite direction because of the rotation of the earth.

Even though the earth turns at the rate of a thousand miles per hour, we do not feel it. The main issue in Christianity is whether or not we are devoted to God, not whether we turn toward God so rapidly that we feel the actual change in the direction of our lives or turn so gradually that we do not.

To insist that everyone must have a conversion experience puts the emphasis on the experience of turning itself, not on the *direction* of a person's life. Whether a commitment to the Christian life takes place suddenly or gradually, it occurs because of the Spirit of God who comes "from above" (John 3:3). There is room in Christ's kingdom for both. For myself, I am glad that I have had such an experience—but it would be better if I were as good a Christian as a friend of mine who has never had a conversion experience yet tells me that she cannot think of a time in her life in which her heart did not respond gladly to stories about Jesus.

In the New Testament there is a great deal of stress on the importance of conversion, since the Christian church was new and without very many members who were born of Christian parents. At first all Christians were Jews who received Jesus as Messiah (Christ) and Lord (a title hitherto reserved for God alone). For them, conversion was not a turn from unbelief to belief, as it so often is with us today, since Jews already believed in God. What they turned from was a community that did not receive Jesus as Messiah and God incarnate to a community that did. At first the church was a community within a larger community. Jewish Christians continued to have their sons circumcised and to worship in the Jewish Temple and synagogues—the larger community—while at the same time they entered the smaller community of Christians through baptism in the name of the Father, Son, and Holy Spirit.

One of the hardest questions for Jewish converts in the early church was the role of the Jewish Law, as evidenced in the many gospel passages where we see Jesus engaged in heated controversy with the Pharisees and the scribes over obedience to the Law. Paul's letters make it clear that not only were gentile, or non-Jewish, converts to Christianity free of obligation to observe the Jewish ritual laws, but so were Jewish Christians, although they might continue to observe practices such as circumcision.

Even more problematic, however, was the place of the Law itself, for according to the Law no one can be judged righteous or just before God. We are so under the power of sin and evil that were God to regard us solely in terms of the requirements of the Law, we would all fail to be pleasing to God. But, as Paul made clear, Jesus Christ justifies us before his Father. God's righteousness is such that God takes into his own life the consequences of our sin and evil by the crucifixion of Jesus, rather than allowing us to suffer the full consequences. God continues to love us and to call on us to enter and follow a path that will allow us to participate in God's life in spite of what we are and what we have done. God takes the death of his Son, a judicial murder, and makes it a holy act. The word *sacrifice* is made up of two Latin words, *sacer* (sacred) and *facere* (to make). God takes Jesus' death and makes it a sacrifice. God does not respond to our rejection of his ways and his intentions by rejecting us; he raises his Son from the dead. It is as if God says, "You just cannot get rid of me, even by killing my Son. Here he is; follow him."

One of the most important consequences of the change in the role of the Law is that Jewish Christians could eat with gentile Christians without defilement. This was a dramatic change, as we can see in the story of Peter's vision and subsequent acceptance of the hospitality of a gentile (Acts 10:9-16). This removal of all barriers between Jew and gentile has been called a "sociological miracle." It is a constant theme of Paul's letter to the Galatians: Jesus has broken down all social division between peoples, and given them an essential unity in Christ.

As many of you as were baptized into Christ have clothed yourselves with Christ. There is no longer Jew or Greek, there is no longer slave or free, there is no longer male and female; for all of you are one in Christ Jesus. (Gal. 3:27-28)

In Christianity there is an invitation by God in Christ to people of all races and classes to join the church as the new Israel.

Gentile converts in the early church were converts from paganism, since atheism as a creed was virtually unknown. Jewish-Christian monotheism was not merely the opposite of pagan polytheism, however, with the former believing in only one God and the latter worshiping many divinities. To think that "gods" is, so to speak, the plural for "God" fails to take into account the fact that the Jewish-Christian God is the source of the universe, whereas the pagan gods were merely part of the universe.

So although these people were not converted from atheism, in Christianity they encountered for the first time something utterly new. They turned not only from the worship of gods, but also from thinking of the universe as something permanent, without beginning or end, which housed both human beings and gods. The latter view was true of the pagan philosophers as well, including those who had little use for the popular civic gods like Zeus or Apollo. Unlike Jews who became Christians, gentile converts learned for the first time that the universe was utterly dependent on God for its existence and order, that God was utterly complete and sufficient without any universe at all, and that it was by God's goodness alone that the universe existed.

Civic religion formed the public worship of gentile people. But alongside civic religion there flourished many mystery cults, whose central feature was the promise of life after death. Each cult claimed to provide its adherents with a secret knowledge (*gnosis*) that was given only to its members. We know little of these cults, but to turn from one of these to Christianity was to turn from secret rituals to what was freely shared, namely, knowledge of Jesus Christ as savior. Rituals and incantations were not a substitute for moral and spiritual regeneration.

One of the great appeals of Christianity for gentiles, who were deeply troubled by the idea of death, was the promise of the resurrection of the dead through union with Christ. Baptism was to die with Christ and to rise with him from the dead. The eucharist, which was at the center of Christian worship, was referred to as "the medicine of immortality" because it healed the damage done to us by sin and gave communion with the living Christ.

Besides turning from the civic gods as powers within the universe to God as creator, and from promises of salvation from death to Jesus as savior, converts turned from immorality to the demanding ethical standards taught by Jesus and exemplified in his own life. Paul's letters are full of rebukes to members of the new Christian churches for their immoral, quarrelsome, and lax behavior, explaining that such actions are utterly incompatible with the new life given to them by Christ. Of course not all gentiles were immoral or lax. Philosophers in the ancient world usually practiced a disciplined and austere life, and they were respected by both pagans and Christians.

Stoicism, the most widespread of all the philosophies, was practiced by many who were not philosophers and, as we will see, its ascetical disciplines influenced the desert fathers and mothers of the fourth century. Nonetheless, Stoic asceticism differed from Christianity in its fundamental aim and purpose, for its goal was self-mastery as an end in itself, while Christians sought control of their passions in order to love their neighbor. In Christianity there was no room for the Stoic ideal of independence from all external circumstances and indifference to external matters. Rather, the Christian sought to be fully dependent on God, who enabled one to love both God and neighbor. For the Christian, pride in one's self-sufficiency was the central sin. So conversion for some pagans was from immorality, and for others from autonomy to dependence on God's love and mercy.

In time, as more and more educated people were converted to Christianity, it became common to draw comparisons between the philosophic understanding of life and the universe and Christian teachings. Justin Martyr, a trained philosopher of the second century, revealed that part of the reason he became a Christian was that Christ bestowed a wisdom superior to that of the philosophers. Using the Bible as a guide and standard, Christian theologians educated in Greek and Roman civilization, such as Origen, Basil the Great, and Augustine, sought to meet the intellectual challenges of a pagan understanding of the meaning and purpose of life with an intellectually satisfying Christian philosophy.

ゝ: ゝ

From this brief survey we can see that what people are converted *from* and what they are converted *to* is not the same in every case, either in the ancient world or today. Today people tend to be converted from disbelief—whether agnosticism or atheism—to belief in God. Atheism is not widespread in the western world, but our intellectual culture is largely secular. A secular outlook is normative, so for an educated person to become a Christian is to move away from what is considered an intellectual norm to a different set of standards and norms entirely. Our educational institutions and research centers approach and teach all subjects and issues without any religious or spiritual reference. As Richard Swinburne, an Oxford philosopher of religion, observed about his education and upbringing,

> My home, my school, my military service...and above all my university were all highly intellectual places, where I was exposed to all the achievements and current attitudes of the modern academic world. These attitudes were, it seemed to me, basically anti-Christian. The ethics of sophisticated intellectuals were very different from the ethics of traditional Christians.[1]

Even though what we are converted from and to is not identical in all times and places, there is a remarkable overlap when we approach conversion from the point of view of the third question we ask of the spiritual life: *What motivates us to begin to follow the Christian path?* Here we find that motives cluster around three major features of Christianity that attract many people: God's power, goodness, and wisdom. Some people are motivated to turn to God because they seek *help* with various kinds of distress; others are drawn by the hope of *nourishment* for a hunger that nothing can satisfy; still others are attracted by the *understanding* of themselves and their world given by the Christian vision. Even in those cases in which one of the three motives is primary, the others may be significantly operative as well. Let us examine each of them in some detail.

Throughout the ages, the most familiar motive that has led people to look to God for help is various kinds of distress. Supernatural power is sought in the face of external dangers such as diseases, storms and droughts, military invasions, and death. At a deeper level supernatural power is sought because of a destructive addiction, or as in the case of Augustine, inability to control one's passions Many people turn to religion because they have found relief for their distress, especially their lack of self-control. Today this is most obvious in Twelve Step programs, where the essential ingredient is a confession of one's own powerlessness in the face of a particular addiction. Someone who has been through the degradation and pain of alcoholism, and who through a spiritual path has found the ability to put a broken and snarled life back together, has very good reason to be religious.

By and of itself relief from suffering does not establish that there is a God, but it is a powerful motive for *belief* in God. Supernatural relief has always been regarded as a reason to be committed and grateful to God—as in Psalm 107, where God is praised because he delivers "from their distress" those who suffer from lack of food and drink, from physical oppression, illness, and storms at sea. The account of the people of Israel is a witness to us—an invitation—to consider walking the path they have walked because, among other things, they have found guidance for life and relief in their distress. As Psalm 107 concludes, "Let those who are wise give heed to these things" (vs. 43).

The second type of motivation is *aspiration.* Many people desire to act justly and they feel guilty over their failures. Frequently in some important respect they have failed their children, or parents, or siblings, or spouse. Reasons for guilt may become a very heavy burden, even in an age in which it is said that shame is replacing guilt and that all values are human projections or the product of power relations within a society. Speaking personally, such speculations do not bring me the slightest relief or incline me to think I have not failed those I love in many ways. I expect the same is true of others, which is why one of the most powerful attractions of Christianity is Jesus' treatment of people who have failed and his teachings about the mercy of God for those who repent.

Part of what lies behind this attraction is our desire to see the vindication of those who are victims of social injustice. One of the burning questions of the Old Testament is, why do the righteous suffer, and the wicked prosper? Although the Bible does not give a complete answer, it does assure us that however much justice is perverted in this life, there is a last judgment at which justice will prevail.

This assurance indicates the ambivalent nature of justice. Our demand that social and personal wrongs be put right requires those of us who are guilty of wrongdoing to suffer for our misdeeds. Today many of us claim to be victims because we are dissatisfied with our social status, our income, or our lot in life, but even if we are victims of serious injustice, we probably are guilty of committing injustice as well. If we are genuinely committed to justice, we ought to wish that the consequences of all the wrong we have done should fall solely on ourselves, not on others. That would be just. It does not take much reflection for us to realize that we do not really want true justice, and indeed we fear it.

Maximus the Confessor points out in his preface to *Four Hundred Chapters on Love* that one of the reasons we turn to God with faith is fear of punishment. To turn to God because of a fear of punishment means that we recognize the fairness of punishment, and realize that if justice is fully carried out, we have a great deal to fear. But we turn to God because God, who is just, is also merciful. God allows the consequences of our actions to fall on himself in the death of Jesus. That is how God shows us the ugly effects of evil so that we will repent of it and receive his love in spite of our deeds.

Because of the validity of justice we realize that we are always dependent on God's mercy, with no grounds for feeling superior to anyone. In this way, our fear of God's punishment and the gift of his mercy can lead us to be grateful to God and to forgive our neighbor as well. This connection is very explicit in Jesus' parable of a man who had debts so great that he could not pay them. Out of mercy his debts were completely remitted, but when he refused to forgive a very small debt that another owed him, he was cast in prison until he should forgive his fellow debtor from his heart (Matt. 18:23-35).

Maximus the Confessor stresses another major aspiration: a hunger for good. Jesus taught us that however good the world is, we "do not live by bread alone" (Matt. 4:4). However much we possess, it is not enough to give us more than temporary satisfaction. Sooner or later we want something else or something more. Unfortunately, this hunger can keep us in the vain pursuit of earthly goods as if they alone could satisfy us, or cause us to lose hope when we realize that we cannot find fullness through them. Maximus advised us that we are indeed to contemplate the goodness of the world, and to enjoy it, but warned that its very inability to satisfy us should make us aware that we have been made for something more. Accordingly, in order to motivate us to seek God, Maximus wrote,

> If all things have been made by God...then God is better than what has been made by him. The one who forsakes the better and is engrossed in inferior things shows that he prefers the things made by God to God himself.[2]

When we consider how wonderful the world is, we ought also to remember how much more wonderful its source is. We need to allow the hunger for good that leads us to enjoy the creation also to lead us to recognize its inability to satisfy us, for only a good that is greater than this world truly can.

When a fifteenth-century spiritual writer like Thomas à Kempis speaks of "contempt for the vanities of this world," it should not be understood as a rejection of the goodness of God's creation or a prohibition against enjoyment of it. Rather, it is to awaken us to the hunger we have for good that is greater than the good of this world, precisely because we have been created to find our goal in sharing in the life of God. God draws us to himself through what we lack, but we have to be attentive in order to be aware of this lack and so allow God's Word in Christ to guide us to his presence. Few people can hear Augustine's words, "Our hearts are restless until they find rest in thee," with utter equanimity.

The third feature in Christianity that attracts and motivates is the *understanding* it gives us of ourselves and our world. Sometimes we find spiritual writers who express hostility and even contempt not only for "worldly learning" but even for theological inquiry as well. This dismissal of the intellect is understandable when those engaged in inquiry forget its purposes, as did many theologians in the late middle ages after the decline of scholasticism. Textbook logic and controversy for its own sake, with greater and greater refinements and increasingly remote speculations, seemed destructive of the spiritual life. This attitude toward scholasticism was certainly prominent in the influential spiritual renewal movement known as the *Devotio Moderna* of the fourteenth and fifteenth centuries, while Luther and Calvin frequently gave voice to it in the sixteenth century. Yet clearly the Reformers did not reject all learning, and even among anti-intellectuals today Christianity appeals to a desire to find some meaning and pattern to life and gain self-understanding.

It is in this third area that Christianity has become vulnerable in modern times. Many people who are otherwise attracted to Christianity because of a need for help, a desire for justice, or a hunger for mercy are still unable to follow Christ. What holds them back is the thoroughly secular understanding of life that is normative for our culture and rejects belief in God in the name of reason and human progress. It is the familiar clash between heart and head.

Two major forces have contributed to a secular worldview: the conviction that morals and society do not need a religious foundation, and the overriding drive toward material progress. With the discovery that people could and did lead good and moral lives without being religious, on the one hand, and the new emphasis on improving the material conditions of human life through science on the other, the spiritual condition of men and women was considered of less and less significance. What developed instead was a type of humanism that saw itself both as alternative to and incompatible with Christianity.

That is why for many intellectuals in the late nineteenth and early twentieth centuries conversion was the recovery of a spiritual perspective that could satisfy the heart *and* the understanding. Converts like Leo Tolstoy, T. S. Eliot, Henri Bergson, Gabriel Marcel, Edith Stein, and Simone Weil had to turn away from the secularity that had come to dominate intellectual culture. The following description from Simone Weil's spiritual autobiography, *Waiting for God,* is quite typical of their experience:

As soon as I reached adolescence, I saw the problem of God as a problem the data of which could not be obtained here below, and I decided that the only way of being sure not to reach the wrong solution, which seemed to me the greatest possible evil, was to leave it alone. So I left it alone. I neither affirmed nor denied anything. It seemed to me useless to solve the problem, for I thought that, being in this world, our business was to adopt the best attitude with regard to the problems of this world, and that such an attitude did not depend upon the solution of the problem of God.[3]

Each of the intellectuals I mentioned describes his or her own journey from this normative secularity to a spiritual perspective in which all things are viewed in a religious light. For all of them the question of intellectual integrity was uppermost, which is why these accounts are particularly valuable to us in shedding light on many of the hindrances to conversion we experience simply through living in modern secular societies. In the next chapter we will examine the conversions of three of these figures: Leo Tolstoy, T. S. Eliot, and Simone Weil.

Notes

1. Quoted in Kelly James Clark, ed., *Philosophers Who Believe* (Madison, Wis.: InterVarsity Press, 1993), 179-180.

2. Maximus the Confessor, *Four Hundred Chapters on Love,* George C. Berthold, trans. (Mahwah, N. J.: Paulist Press, 1985), 1.5.

3. Simone Weil, *Waiting for God* (New York: Harper & Row, 1973), 62.

CHAPTER FOUR

THREE JOURNEYS TO GOD

The ways in which God's power, goodness, and truth make themselves felt in people's lives and lead to their conversion differ considerably. Accordingly, we will examine three people's experiences of the reality of God and see how they moved from a secular to a spiritual point of view in understanding themselves and the world. All three were highly accomplished, well-educated, and critically-minded people: Leo Tolstoy, one of the greatest novelists of the nineteenth century; T. S. Eliot, one of the most influential British poets of the twentieth century; and Simone Weil, a French philosopher and political activist of the 1930s. Their religious traditions were, respectively, Russian Orthodoxy, Anglicanism, and Roman Catholicism.

Tolstoy has left a full account of his recovery of commitment to the Christian faith, which he had discarded as a young man at university. For about a year, he wrote, "My heart was oppressed by a tormenting feeling, which I cannot describe as otherwise than as a searching after God."[1] In any search we are looking for what we do not have. Erich Maria Remarque, author of *All Quiet on the Western Front,* in his lesser known novel *Night Out of Lisbon,* ironically compares people who think they wish to seek God to people who say they want to learn how to swim—but who insist on remaining fully clothed, with hat, overcoat, gloves, and heavy shoes, a bulging suitcase in each hand and a knapsack on their backs.

Just as we must strip off our clothing and other impediments in order to learn how to swim, in order to seek God we must set aside the idea that the things of this world can give us complete and lasting satisfaction. Our need for God, which causes us to feel dissatisfied with life, does not always reach the intensity of torment, as it did for Tolstoy, but without some awareness that something vital to life is missing, the search for God is not an authentic one. If we feel no lack, then we do not seek; if we do not seek, we are unlikely to find God.

"This search," Tolstoy continues, "was not an act of my reason, but a feeling, and I say this advisedly, because it was opposed to my way of thinking; it came from the heart. It was a feeling of dread, of orphanhood, of isolation amid things all apart from me, and of hope in a help I knew not from whom." The life God intends us to have implies that our present life, for all its goodness, is by itself inadequate. Our awareness of its inadequacies fills us with dread, especially when we consider the inevitability of suffering, the loss of loved ones, and the prospect of our own death. Feeling "orphaned" is the result of not having yet come to a spiritual point of reference that would enable us to find our place in God's order. A secular orientation, however successful it may be in giving us a sense of status and significance in the social order, cannot satisfy our craving for a proper self-understanding or cure our sense of isolation.

Part of the motive behind his conversion was that Tolstoy, like many other people, came to crave a sense of purpose and direction. Yet Tolstoy's search for God could not be an act of reason:

> Though I was well convinced of the impossibility of proving the existence of God—Kant had shown me, and I had thoroughly grasped his reasoning, that this did not admit of proof—I still sought to find a God, still hoped to do so, and still, from the force of former habits, addressed myself to one in prayer. Him whom I sought, however, I did not find.

Like many intellectuals of his time, he had accepted Immanuel Kant's refutations of the so-called traditional proofs for God's existence and believed that the only way to establish the reality of God was by rational proof.

It was Tolstoy's previous religious training ("the force of former habits") that finally enabled him to find a way to God through prayer. Apparently, he did not realize that he was actually following the path frequently recommended by spiritual guides, such as Teresa of Avila, a sixteenth-century reformer of the church in Spain and the founder of many religious communities. In *The Interior Castle,* her great book on the spiritual life, Teresa compares the human personality to a castle with many rooms. One of these rooms contains the image of God. Even though it is the most lovely room of all in the castle, many of us occupy far inferior quarters, smeared with filth and dirt, so that our likeness to God is impossible to recognize.

The way to enter the loveliest room of the castle is by prayer. When Tolstoy began to pray he found that his prayers were not answered immediately:

> The more I prayed, the clearer it became that I was not heard, that there was no one to whom to pray. With despair in my heart that there was no God, I cried, "Lord, have mercy on me, and save! O Lord, my God, teach me!" But no one had mercy on me, and I felt that life stood still within me.

But Tolstoy's need for God, which included his need for significance and purpose, enabled him to persevere and eventually find that his prayers had an effect. "*He is,* I said to myself. I had only to admit that for an instant to feel that life re-arose in me, to feel the possibility of existing and the joy of it."

The sheer affirmation of God's existence deeply moved Tolstoy because he was so seriously engaged with the question of the reality of God. Often our words and prayers do not have a comparable effect on us because our attention is not focused on God. We violate the commandment "You shall not take the name of the Lord your God in vain" (Exod. 20:7) by invoking God's name frivolously. The ineffectiveness of our words and prayers can be compared to the ineffectiveness of racing a car engine. All drivers know that unless the gears are engaged by moving the gear lever the car will not move, however much they step on the accelerator. The engine will simply whirl around faster. So too with our talking and praying. Unless we are seriously engaged with the reality of God, our words and thoughts are in vain. They do not move us, as did Tolstoy's words and prayers, from distress to joy.

Even though Tolstoy's words and prayers led him to joy, this result was not of itself sufficient to give him a lasting conviction of the reality of God. Next he was led to question whether his joy in the affirmation of God was merely the product of his own mental processes. "Reason continued his work," he said, and reason said to him,

> "The conception of God is not God. Conception is what goes on within myself; the conception of God is an idea which I am able to rouse in my mind or not as I choose; it is not what I seek, something without which life could not be." Then again all seemed to die around and within me, and again I wished to kill myself.

These doubts only began to give way when Tolstoy became clearer in his own mind what finding God meant:

> I began to retrace the process which had gone on within myself, the hundred times repeated discouragement and revival. I remembered that I had lived only when I believed in a God. As it was before, so it was now; I had only to know God, and I lived; I had only to forget Him, not to believe in Him, and I died. What was this discouragement and revival? I do not live when I lose faith in the existence of a God; I should long ago have killed myself, if I had not had a dim hope of finding Him. I only really live when I feel and seek Him. "What more, then, do I seek?" A voice seemed to cry within me, "This is He, He without whom there is no life. To know God and to live are one. God is life."

To know God and to live are one because God is *zoe*, the uncreated life. God the Holy Spirit is an indwelling presence whose manifestations can be mistaken for simple human elation. This is what Tolstoy thought at first, until he recognized that God is life and God's presence can become an habitual one, which requires only our attention to give us a permanent peace and joy. With this realization the cycle of misery and elation ceased, and the light that shone on him never left him again.

Since God seeks us first, we do not need to rely on arguments for God's existence; knowledge of God is possible through conscious *interaction* with God. To experience the effects of the divine life in our own can lead to a firm belief in the reality of God. The reason why religious faith is not mere credulity is that it is anchored in the uncreated life of God, often referred to as grace or the Holy Spirit. More than this simple contact is needed to produce rational conviction, as we will see even more clearly in Simone Weil's account of her spiritual journey, but it is because of grace that we first enter the path that leads to conviction.

Conversion cannot be reduced to "good feelings," however, because feelings alone will not lead us to change the way we live. To interact with God is to recognize that our lives must be transformed and become increasingly like God's life. One way of recognizing that our religious feelings are the result of interacting with God is that we find ourselves seeking to have our lives conform to his.[2] Therefore when Tolstoy came to explicit faith in God, he had the simultaneous conviction that he should obey God's will.

It was strange, but this feeling of the glow of life was no new sensation; it was old enough, for I had been led away from it in the earlier part of my life....I returned to faith in that Will which brought me into being and which required something of me; I returned to the belief that the one single aim in life should be...to live in accordance with that Will;...in other words, I returned to a belief in God.

The path we follow to achieve contact with God need not be precisely the same as the one Tolstoy followed, but we have examined his carefully because it contains many features common to the lives of people who have come to faith in God:

first, a conscious need for God and the beginning of a search for him;

second, barriers to belief in God that put the seeker in a quandary, whether it is the notion that science has made belief in God implausible or doubts about the trustworthiness of the Bible or lack of confidence in the credibility of the church's teachings;

third, the mitigation or removal of these barriers by a greater understanding of what Christianity teaches;

fourth, the need to go beyond understanding to prayer;

fifth, a pattern of oscillation back and forth between a sense of conviction, even certainty, and doubt, which is commonly found in accounts of pilgrimages to a firm and settled faith; and

sixth, increased clarity about what it means to recognize that to be spiritually nourished by Christian teachings, worship, and devotion is to be in contact with God. This recognition of God's reality includes a desire to live in accordance with God's will, and usually brings a stability that can weather moments or even long periods of doubt, distraction in prayer, and barrenness of spirit.

❧   ❧

The journey of T. S. Eliot to religious faith was very different from that of Tolstoy. For Eliot and many of his generation, the horrors of World War I shattered any dreams of progress through science and education. This sense of disillusionment meant that people were increasingly left without any tradition whatsoever, secular or Christian. Eliot's description of the recovery of religious tradition does include, like Tolstoy's, an intensely personal journey, but his account focuses less on the individual and more on the larger body of people who participate in the invisible and visible body of Christ, the church. The recovery of tradition is necessary, as Eliot states near the end of *Four Quartets*, because "a people without history is not redeemed by time."

Eliot saw the utopian aspirations of the twenties and thirties as the faint awareness of a paradise we might have had, but lost. The intellectual challenge of the present, which results from the collapse of our secular and religious traditions, make our restoration particularly difficult. But every age, even pious ones with a living tradition, have difficulty in finding God, as we see reflected in St. Anselm's prayer of the twelfth century, "O Lord my God, teach my heart where and how to seek you, and where and how to find you."[3] But people who live in an age without tradition, guided by momentary fashions, have an additional difficulty. We do not encounter as a matter of course anything that *explicitly* calls our attention to those questions in life that will give us an opening to the eternal. The loss of tradition means, therefore, that the way to God will not be simple or quick, but will require an extensive and strenuous search.

Eliot spent many years studying Indic religious philosophy, seeking to determine whether mystical experience provided a route to redemption. By the time he came to write *Four Quartets*, he had decided that unless these intense, private experiences were connected to history and thus to Christian doctrines rooted in events such as the incarnation, crucifixion, and resurrection of Jesus, they were merely deceptive. In a similar way Eliot dismissed all quick solutions, whether passing fads, unreflective piety, or shallow mysticism. For him the route to our redemption was analogous to the way of negation, the *via negativa*, of Christian spirituality.

In section three of the first quartet, *Burnt Norton*, Eliot begins with the words "This is the place of disaffection" and goes on to describe the twilight that envelops us when we renounce the hope that the world has saving value. As the poem continues we go deeper into the darkness. For Eliot the path is not the negation or rejection of every image or idea of God as less than God, as in the way of negation, but a rejection of every hope. Eliot was well aware of the disillusionment that followed the collapse of German and British idealism, and other such attempts to discern an immanent pattern in history. Such disillusionment was only a half-darkness, however, a partial renunciation, and was not the complete purgation required by the way of negation. We must enter a deep darkness in which we become fully aware of our sinful presumption and our powerlessness. Eliot is speaking of a darkness that can be found in any age and culture because it is the result not only of the human incapacity to grasp God with the senses or the intellect, as in the way of negation, but an awareness of our inability to save ourselves.

Disillusionment and even atheism may be useful preliminaries for a search for God. According to Eliot, however, we must descend lower—into the far greater darkness—if the darkness of the present age is to assist in our purgation and the recovery of the Christian tradition by our society. Eliot is describing the need to endure the distress of life without the meaning, joy, and hope that Tolstoy experienced. He is not simply describing what he personally had to undergo, for he believed our entire culture must undergo a period of purgation in order to be able to receive its heritage, in order to find a redemption from its disillusionment.

For Eliot there is no direct way home. Sinning is necessary. We must pass through the thinking of our age, an age that claims both ultimacy and the loss of it. Healing comes when we take responsibility for our own condition and our own past. The time that seemed wasted and futile is now redeemed, connected to the eternal in repentance; motives and aim are purified. The way takes the seeker through the loss of ultimacy in the seeker's own personal and our cultural history.

When we repent, reconnecting with our past through confession of our sin, we gain a future. By repentance we may now move forward. We now have the world we renounced; although it did not possess ultimacy before, when we saw it only from our old point of view, it now has significance and goodness for us. We find all that we are and all we possess by the suffering of the crucified Word of God. We now have the world restored to us as God's creatures, and all human achievement is placed under God's providential care.

Eliot's account of a conversion that is fully imbedded in history and culture is particularly relevant today because we tend to think of conversion solely in personal terms. Eliot makes us see that conversion is indeed intensely personal, but it also involves turning our backs on the old order and turning toward the new. Eliot helps us see beyond the limited horizons of our own present, although the journey to a new perspective is never short or painless for those who seek understanding.

⌣ ∿

Simone Weil was a contemporary of T. S. Eliot's, although she died toward the end of the Second World War. Earlier in her life she had considered the problem of God to be both insoluble and irrelevant, but that was before she was converted to religious faith through a series of three extraordinary experiences that she relates in her autobiography, *Waiting for God.* Hers is a compelling example of the conversion of the understanding and has much to tell us about holding to Christian doctrines with intellectual integrity. Her conversion shares some of the features we have examined in Tolstoy's conversion, but her initial experience of the reality of God was not, like his, the result of a conscious search.

Her first contact with Catholicism occurred after a bout of ill health following a year of factory work, which she had undertaken voluntarily to understand better the nature of affliction. She was taken by her parents to recuperate in Portugal and there she witnessed a religious procession in a very poor fishing village. The heart-rending sadness of the hymns filled her with the conviction "that Christianity is preeminently the religion of slaves," suitable only for those who are wretched. Some time later, while visiting the church in Assisi where St. Francis often prayed, she was overwhelmed by its incomparable purity and later wrote that "something stronger than I was compelled me for the first time in my life to go down on my knees."[4] Through this experience, Weil found for the first time that such a compulsion could be elevating rather than degrading, unlike her experience of factory work.

Finally, at the abbey church of Solesmes, while attending services in Holy Week, she simultaneously experienced the burden of a splitting headache and a pure and perfect joy in the beauty of the chanting and the words of the service: "It goes without saying that in the course of these services the thought of the Passion of Christ entered into my being once and for all." These experiences, coupled with the reading of the English metaphysical poets whose works she discovered at Solesmes, gave her a view of Christianity as a religion primarily for those who are wretched. The believer finds a force in Christianity that is elevating, but elevation comes in the midst of suffering. Weil was particularly struck by George Herbert's poems, especially the poem from *The Temple* entitled "Love (III)," and used to recite it when she was suffering from violent headaches. This led to her experience of what in spiritual theology is called a divine visitation:

> Often at the culminating point of a violent headache, I make myself say it over, concentrating all my attention upon it and clinging with all my soul to the tenderness it enshrines. I used to think I was merely reciting it as a beautiful poem, but without my knowing it the recitation had the virtue of a prayer. It was during one of these recitations that, as I told you, Christ himself came down and took possession of me.

In contrast to Tolstoy, who searched out and found God, in Weil's case God found her. It is critical that her mystical experience occurred when she was reciting *Love* because the poem is about Jesus sacrificing himself for those who are wretched and offering his crucified body as a banquet of food to nourish them. Weil was able to identify the love by which she was possessed as the presence of Christ, because of the love of Christ that the poem presents. It is the intersection of wretchedness and elevation by love that is the core of her three significant experiences with Christianity. The Christ who takes possession of her is one in whom affliction and love intersect.

"In all my arguments about the insolubility of the problem of God," Weil wrote of this experience later, "I had never foreseen the possibility of that, of a real contact, person to person, here below, between a human being and God." However, she then goes on to make a distinction that is of crucial importance: "Yet I still half refused, not my love but my intelligence. For it seemed to me certain, and I still think so today, that one can never wrestle enough with God if one does so out of pure regard for the truth."

In other words, Weil does not regard her mystical experience as sufficient in itself to establish the reality of God or the truth of Christian doctrines. Thus she does not follow the common route found in the philosophy of religion, which focuses exclusively on the religious experience itself in order to see if it is sufficient to establish either the reality of God or the truth of Christian doctrines. Nor does she claim that mystical experience is the source or the replacement for Christian doctrines, as mystics are commonly thought to claim. Instead, rather than relying on her religious experience as conclusive proof for the existence of God, Weil engages in intellectual work in order fully to convince her mind of the reality of God. Her method is to use the intersection of wretchedness and love as a key to understanding Christian doctrines; in turn, these doctrines are used to illuminate such things as self-regard, personal relations, society, the natural world, suffering, war, work, and beauty.

Hence it was not her mystical experience as such that convinced Weil, but the light it was able to shed on Christian doctrines and, subsequently, the light these doctrines shed elsewhere:

If I light an electric torch at night, I don't judge its power by looking at the bulb, but by seeing how many objects it lights up....The brightness of a source of light is appreciated by the illumination it projects upon non-luminous objects....The value of a religious or, more generally, a spiritual way of life is appreciated by the amount of illumination thrown upon the things of this world.[5]

Weil's intellectual work is directed toward giving human beings nourishment through contact with God; in this she is very much in the ancient and medieval theological tradition in which theology is to help us increase our knowledge and love of God. To know God is to know "the things of this world" as they are related to a divine, suffering love and manifest God's glory. The Christian doctrines of creation, incarnation, and trinity, as well as the sacraments of baptism and eucharist, are "mysteries" that lie beyond the mind's power to comprehend fully. Nonetheless we can love these mysteries and, because they cast light on the things of this world, they increase our understanding of God, our world, and ourselves.

All our intellectual work is guided by the light shed by the love of these Christian mysteries. For example, we may analyze politics and the social order in this light. Because of God's desire to dwell in every person, human beings are ends instead of means, and they have a dignity that cannot be affected by injury or loss of social position or even death. Human dignity is in turn the basis for our legal system and virtually every ethical theory in western civilization, including humanism.

In theology and the philosophy of religion, the dominant focus is usually the relationship of faith and reason; in Weil, however, the focus is *love*, faith, and reason. The mysteries of religion are above reason, and therefore faith by itself would simply be an attachment based on our needs and desires. But when loved with a pure love—one that does not seek consolation or gain—these mysteries illuminate those places that are otherwise dark and disconnected. For example, Weil points out the resemblance between human love, which is shown in loving our neighbor, and divine love, which is revealed in the Christian doctrines of creation, incarnation, crucifixion, and trinity. We can tell from their behavior and attitudes toward others whether people are in contact with the supernatural, but *in themselves* such acts are not sufficient for us to say that love of neighbor is a revelation of supernatural love. Something more is needed. We may not at first realize that God is behind our loving our neighbor because, as Weil says, "It does not rest with the soul to believe in the reality of God if God does not reveal this reality."[6] Direct contact with God of some kind is needed in order for us to say with certainty and intellectual honesty that the love of neighbor reveals divine love or, to put it another way, that love of neighbor is one of the "implicit forms" of the love of God.

Weil also explains how we may have direct contact with God that is not, as in her own case, a mystical experience. Even though God alone can reveal God's reality, it does lie within our power to be aware that we are hungry for a final and ultimate good and to know that all that we love falls short of it. If we continue to hunger, God the Holy Spirit, in God's own good time, begins to nourish us with a gracious presence. We become convinced that it is a *supernatural* love that nourishes us through all the kinds of loves human beings are capable of: love of neighbor, love of the beauty of the world, love of religious ceremonies, and the love found in friendship. All four loves Weil called "forms of the implicit love of God," and all four have a supernatural source.

In this final section on Simone Weil I have stressed the role of understanding in the mind's coming to a sense of firm conviction of the truth of the Christian vision, for that is how many have found their path to God. It is important that Christianity make intellectual sense so that emotions are not the only basis for being a Christian. But if such understanding is all that Christianity has to offer, then it is merely an intellectual option. Christianity's appeal to the understanding has to be balanced by a reaching out to God in prayer. However natural it is to seek to enlarge our understanding of God through our mind, Christianity is not merely an intellectual option. It also meets our needs in distress and satisfies our hunger for justice and goodness. Only then do we know God's presence in our lives.

Notes

1. Leo Tolstoy, *My Confession* (New York: Thomas Y. Crowell, 1887). Tolstoy's account of this period in his life is drawn from pages 103-108.

2. For a philosophical defense of the reasonableness of relying on contact with God and the reasons to believe that we are in contact with God, see my book *The Reasonableness of Faith* (Washington, D.C.: Corpus Books, 1968), especially chapter 5. It can also be found in my article "Motives, Reasons, and Rationales" in *American Philosophical Quarterly* (April 1966).

3. *The Prayers and Meditations of Saint Anselm*, Benedicta Ward, SLG, trans. (Harmondsworth, England: Penguin, 1973), 239-240.

4. Simone Weil, *Waiting for God* (New York: Harper & Row, 1973). This account of her conversion can be found on pages 64-69.

5. *The Simone Weil Reader*, George Panichas, ed. (New York: David McKay, 1981), 417-418.

6. Weil, *Waiting for God*, 211.

CHAPTER FIVE

THE EIGHT DEADLY THOUGHTS

What can a Christian do to become more loving? As we saw in the last chapter, although Leo Tolstoy assumed his conversion was the terminus of his journey to love of God and love of neighbor, actually it was only the beginning. He made the mistake of thinking that he could go directly from his conversion to love of neighbor. Many Christians do not have a sudden and powerful conversion experience like Tolstoy's, so they enter the Christian life having already developed some of the virtues that make love of neighbor possible. Nonetheless, all Christians find that they continually fail to obey Christ's commandments, and it troubles them that they do not love their neighbors as themselves and do not love God with all their heart, mind, soul, and strength. They know that they are forgiven through Christ for their failures, and they are reminded of this at every service of worship. Still, the question remains: what can Christians do to grow in love of God and neighbor?

The branch of theology devoted to specifying the major hindrances to Christian love and the practices to overcome them is called ascetical theology. In this chapter I will draw on a small part of the ascetical teachings of the fourth-century desert fathers and mothers who lived in the wildernesses of Egypt and Syria, and will look for ways they can help us today. Particularly valuable is their treatment of the most common and basic things with which all human beings have to deal: food and drink, sexual desires, material goods, the need to compare ourselves to others, resentment, failure, success, and self-centeredness. The temptations these give rise to were traditionally called "the eight deadly thoughts." Everyone is attacked by them, and unless we develop some control over them, we are deeply hindered from growing in Christian love.

The teachings of the desert hermits were first codified in two books called *On Practice* and *Chapters on Prayer*, written in the fourth century by a monastic scholar named Evagrius. Originally from Pontus, a Roman province on the Black Sea in what is now northeastern Turkey, Evagrius was a friend and pupil of the Cappadocian Fathers, who were the principal theologians of the Nicene Creed and orthodox trinitarian faith. Basil the Great ordained him to be a lector (a minor order leading to priesthood), while Gregory of Nazianzen, bishop of Constantinople, the imperial capital, raised him to the diaconate and made him his archdeacon. Evagrius proved to be a brilliant assistant, a fine preacher, and an able defender of the trinitarian faith against heresy. At the Second General Council of 381 he also became acquainted with Gregory of Nyssa, who profoundly and permanently influenced his theological outlook.

In the course of his ecclesiastical career, Evagrius fell passionately in love with a married woman. In a dream he was warned by an angel of great danger and, even though innocent of any wrongdoing, he vowed to leave his important post at the center of power in Constantinople to become a monastic in Egypt. There his love of learning, which had made abandonment of the intellectual life of the imperial city so painful, enabled him to sift and organize the rich experience and sayings of the desert hermits into what became classic works that profoundly shaped Christian spirituality. These teachings reached the Latin-speaking church in the West in a vastly augmented form through John Cassian in his *Conferences* and *Institutes;* subsequently, during the sixth century, Gregory the Great revised the concept of the eight deadly thoughts and called them instead the seven deadly sins.

The earlier tradition of Evagrius and Cassian, however, stresses that what human beings wrestle with are not sins so much as *thoughts* which stir up passions and cause emotional turmoil. We are not evil people just because we find ourselves thinking these "deadly thoughts"—in fact, the eight deadly thoughts are modeled on the temptations Christ faced in the wilderness, and every Christian can expect sooner or later to be assailed by them in seeking to follow Christ. But unless some mastery of these deadly thoughts is achieved, we will be tempted by them into sin. Even when we do not commit sins, our unruly passions seriously hinder us from following Christ. These passions are easily aroused, and we are so constantly distracted in our struggle with them that we are unable to be attentive to others or to grow in our awareness of God's presence.

Evagrius does not attempt to give a full account of the human passions he examines, but treats them only as they hinder us from obeying Christ. Furthermore, he examines our emotions and attitudes in their crudest form: gluttony in relation to food and drink, lust in relation to sexual instinct, avarice in relation to material goods. The development of virtue in ascetical theology is therefore a treatment of only its bare beginnings: learning to avoid the blatant sins that hinder our love of neighbor and hamper our growth in the love of God. The fullness of virtue or excellence that Christians ultimately hope for is a fully realized and restored humanity, which is commonly described as becoming as much like Christ as possible. However, neglecting the rudiments of virtue can have deadly consequences. By destroying our ability to become what we ought to become and can become in Christ, this neglect leaves us under the control of destructive forces.

We may be alarmed to hear that we are to *strive* to become virtuous, since we are taught that we are saved not by our own goodness, but by God's grace alone. Evagrius and other ascetical theologians would certainly agree with this teaching. Maximus the Confessor, a great systematic theologian and teacher of the seventh century, warned his students against the twofold aspect of pride, which would lead monks to take the credit for their own good deeds and so look down upon their less virtuous brothers, rather than offering their thanks to God. Such a monk, wrote Maximus, "is evidently putting himself forward as someone who acts uprightly on his own power; but this is impossible, as the Lord told us, 'Outside of me, you can do nothing.'" [1]

The desert monastics were fully aware of the need for grace; they were preoccupied with the feebleness—or even absence—of the fruits of God's grace in Christ. Ascetical theology is concerned with disciplines and practices that will allow God's grace to become more effective in our lives. These theologians clearly know that the ability to love our neighbors and to love God comes from God, but we can resist and hinder God's grace by our failure to control those desires that awaken our passions. We can become so regularly agitated and stirred up by such things as lust or anger that God's grace does not make us nearly as much like Christ as it otherwise would. As we make the effort to become virtuous, and meet with some success, it becomes easier for us to love our neighbors and God because we suffer from fewer distractions.

The term "ascetical" comes from the Greek *ascesis,* or discipline. St. Paul described the Christian life as a race to be run, requiring training or discipline if it is to be run well. He also pointed out that a boxer must acquire skill in order to fight well. In order to achieve the physical fitness and skill necessary to run or fight well a person must train and practice, and this means to submit to discipline. Paul transferred this obvious physical fact into the spiritual realm. Those who seek to follow Christ, even though forgiven, are still weak and rebellious in various respects. Unless they make the effort to overcome their weaknesses and rebellious attitudes, they will be greatly hampered in their efforts to follow Christ.

❧   ❧

The first of the eight deadly thoughts Evagrius examines concerns our appetite for food. When monastics feel hungry they are often tempted to eat before meal time, he says, or to eat too much, because of the fantasies flashing before their minds of fellow monastics who fasted and became ill. Taking care of one's health can become an excuse for eating at the wrong time or eating more than one needs. We must remember that monastics lived very simply, eating only what was necessary. Part of the reason for this was to develop self-control, which everyone needs, but the main purpose was so that they would have more to share, particularly with the unemployed in cities and with widows and orphans. These monastics did not live on donations; they not only farmed, but also engaged in such craft as making and selling furniture. Evagrius himself, because he was well-educated, copied manuscripts to earn his keep and shared his excess. To limit oneself to necessities, therefore, had the great value of being able to help those in need.

Applied to our own situation, we might say that although Christians are not required to restrict themselves to the bare necessities, our appetite for food and drink is not easy to control. Because the gratification of appetites is pleasurable, we have to make an effort to restrain them. Many of us find it hard to stop eating good food even when we feel full and know that we will regret it later; few of us know when to say, "Enough!" The "deadly thoughts" that assail us are, "Don't be afraid to enjoy yourself!" "Don't deny yourself anything you really want—that is not the way to fulfill yourself!" Gratification is so pleasurable that under the influence of such thoughts we are vulnerable to injuring ourselves and others by simply following our impulses to self-indulgence. In addition, if we cannot control our appetites, it is unlikely that we can ever be strong enough to give up anything for the sake of another person or do something for the sake of another when it runs counter to one of our appetites. Loving our neighbor as ourselves will always be out of our reach.

Evagrius is concerned with our common human nature and the appetites we all share, but he does not consider special or distinctive conditions. For example, some people have been raised in homes that enabled them to develop good eating habits, while others may have developed bad habits of overindulgence because of a parent's encouragement to overeat, or unhealthy habits because of social and peer pressures to be thin. We need to be aware of this dimension, however, because eating disorders, like alcohol abuse, pose a severe social problem. There is a need for serious theological thinking and teaching in churches today on these matters that so greatly affect our lives.[2]

Evagrius' particular value is that he calls attention to the moral and spiritual significance of common, everyday matters with which all of us must deal. Just because we may not be troubled with anorexia or bulimia or some other food-related disorder does not mean that we can ignore our relation to food and drink. Without eating only as much as we need to live, we still can learn to eat more simply in order to have more to share with others.

In addition, developing the discipline to deal with the appetite of hunger helps one to deal with the second deadly thought, lust. Evagrius himself mentions lust only briefly. He simply says that those who practice continence are strenuously assailed by the deadly thought that they should abandon it because "they gain nothing by it." As we might say today, "What is to be gained by denying your desire for another person, when both of you consent and there is no exploitation?" To condemn lust is not to condemn sexual instinct as such. A human being is more than a body, and the body of a human being cannot be separated from the person—from who he or she is. The body is, so to speak, the outside of the soul, the part of the person we can see. To lust is to desire the body of a person, and not the person; lust depersonalizes. Erotic love, in contrast to lust or mere sensuousness, has within its very nature the thought, "I will love you always." Such an erotic love is highly personal and not promiscuous.

George Herbert, the seventeenth-century Anglican poet and priest, points out in his poem "The Church Porch" in *The Temple* that the failure to control the "cheapest sins" has the "dearest" consequences:

The cheapest sins most dearly punisht are,
Because to shun them also is so cheap:
For we have wit to mark them, and to spare.

When we fall under the control of lust or food or drink, further-more, it makes us blind to the goodness of the life God wishes us to have. Blindness results in the deadly thought that there is nothing to be gained by control of our sexual instincts, as Herbert writes of the blindness caused by lust:

> Beware of lust: it doth pollute and foul
> Whom God in Baptism washt with his own blood.
> It blots thy lesson written in thy soul;
> Thy holy lines cannot be understood.
> How dare those eyes upon a Bible look,
> Much less towards God, whose lust is all their book?

The desire for sexual gratification can become such a great and controlling desire that to give it up for any other good, including fidelity, does not appear to be worth it. As Iris Murdoch, the philosopher and novelist, has argued again and again, all that forms and shapes our emotions goes into what we can see and value and what we cannot see or value. Value is not in the eye of the beholder, as those who claim that all values are human projections argue, but what we are able to see does depend largely on our spiritual condition. This is why some self-control in the common areas of life is necessary before we can turn our attention to those things that enable us to know and love God better.

In his *Four Hundred Chapters on Love*, in which he collected in summary form all the Christian teachings on love prior to the seventh century, Maximus the Confessor makes an important distinction in discussing the temptations of lust and anger:

> The mind of the one who loves God does not engage in battle against things nor against their representations, but against the passions joined to these representations. Thus it does not war against the woman nor against the one who offends him, nor against their images, but against the passions that are joined to these images.[3]

The problem lies with the person who feels lustful or takes offense, not with the one who excites the lust or causes the offense. It is a pity that more men do not recognize this distinction, for so much of male hatred for woman is actually the result of disgust with their own lust. One of the dangers of the spiritual life is that in rejecting evil we project it onto others, rather than recognize it in ourselves.

The strict ascetical practices of the desert monks has led to the criticism that they regarded the body itself as evil. As a matter of fact both Evagrius and Cassian had a positive attitude toward the body, regarding it as valuable in enabling spiritual growth. In his *Conferences* John Cassian noted that to have bodies gives human beings a great advantage over pure spirits. Our bodies, he said, can hinder us from carrying out wicked thoughts as soon as they occur—in contrast to pure spirits, for whom the thought is carried out immediately. This delay between conceiving an evil thought and executing it sometimes hinders us from carrying out the evil thought, either because we repent or because some better thought arises. The fact that we are embodied is not an obstacle to be overcome, but a help on the spiritual journey.

In commenting on these theologians' positive attitude toward the body, Owen Chadwick notes that the tension of flesh and spirit furnishes "a sane path to virtue between the warring elements, a royal road, the king's highway. The carnal instincts are good. They are like a good schoolmaster who drives the class to work."[4] The asceticism of the desert monks was not an end in itself, but a means to loving their neighbor and loving God. That we ought not to be doctrinaire in Christian ascetical practices was nicely expressed by John Calvin when he wrote that God created food not only to keep us alive but to give "delight and good cheer," and clothes for "comeliness" as well as warmth and decency, concluding, "Did he not, then, render many things attractive to us, apart from their necessary use?"[5]

~ ~

The third deadly thought concerns avarice, and here Evagrius' comments are surprising. Our need for material goods, he writes in chapter 9 of the *Praktikos*, "suggests to the mind a lengthy old age, inability to perform manual labor (at some future date), famines that are sure to come, sickness that will visit us, the pinch of poverty, the great shame that comes from accepting the necessities of life from others." These thoughts fill us with anxiety and insecurity, and keep us from being generous. Our minds become so full of the desire to gain enough material goods to make ourselves secure against every possible calamity that we fail to pay sufficient attention to either our neighbor or God. Or if we do consider them, we do so largely in terms of how they may help make us financially secure. One of the fruits of the Spirit, indicative of God's activity in our lives, is that we become *like* God—namely, generous.

The next deadly thought, sadness, arises when we compare our achievements with those of others and find we are deeply disappointed with our lives. This sadness is a form of self-pity, which we may experience as we think about what we might have become had we not suffered from the restrictions that come with being a Christian. So rather than finding joy in following Christ's ways, we think of all the pleasures we could have enjoyed were it not for our obedience. The deadly thought of sadness also arises when we ask ourselves, "What might I have become were it not for my brothers and sisters, or my spouse, or my social background, my race, my sex?" These thoughts are frequently accompanied with anger at those whom we hold responsible for the lackluster life in which we now feel trapped, or against those who have or are what we desire. Sadness is a deadly thought, fraught with unrealistic fantasies of how much greater we might have become.

Until I read Evagrius, it had never occurred to me that sadness was a major hindrance to the Christian life. Yet I recalled how I used to read in my college alumni magazine about the achievements of my classmates and would feel depressed about it, and Evagrius helped me to realize how much my opinion about myself is easily affected by comparing myself with others. Many of us are burdened with a great deal of such sadness. It signifies that we still have not fully received the freedom of a Christian who does not live under the bondage of achievement, but whose primary self-understanding and identity is based on God's positive and loving view. Sadness is one of those things I would have overlooked as something of spiritual significance, were it not for the fact that ascetical theology calls attention to it and shows it to be a form of bondage that Christ's love can help us to shed.

The passion of anger can be classified with sadness, since it too is not an appetite but is concerned with our relationships with other people. Evagrius treats only the anger that arises from injuries we have suffered, or think we have suffered, from others, and which can so possess us that anger becomes a permanent disposition, needing very little to set it off. The very thought of those who have hurt us, or who we think have hurt us, fills us with hatred and ignites the burning passion of anger.

Here we must note again that Evagrius is not talking about individual circumstances, which vary widely, but of the injuries that we all experience, and which can cause any of us to become someone who bears grudges and hates another person. Sometimes, however, anger is a healthy response to unfairness and injury. For example, people who have been systematically oppressed are encouraged to feel their anger, which makes sense when anger at the unfairness and the outrages that have been committed has been suppressed. In this case not only is suppressed anger self-destructive, it is unlikely to be open to healing unless it is allowed to come to consciousness. But we cannot stop there, for such felt anger can also become self-destructive. It can lead one to act unjustly as well if it starts to possess our thoughts with the desire for revenge, rather than yielding to a desire for reconciliation.

Even so, the teachings of Christ do not mean that we are simply to take abuse, always and in every circumstance turning the other cheek. For Christ also taught us not to cast our pearls before swine lest they be trampled underfoot. As we seek to be

reconciled instead of responding to our natural desire for revenge, we turn the other cheek when there is real hope of
reconciliation. When we see that others who have injured us
do not respond to our desire for reconciliation, but repeatedly
take advantage of us, those who injure us are like swine,
unresponsive to kindness or appeals to justice. We are not called
by Christ to bear such senseless abuse. Of course, this distinction is easier to state than to recognize in concrete circumstances, and to seek reconciliation is easier said than done. That
is why the deadly thought of anger is taken so seriously by those
who seek to be united with Christ's way, as did the desert
monastics.

⌐ ~

The next three deadly thoughts arise only as we wrestle with
the others, and they all relate to the question of progress in the
Christian life. At first we may be so pleased at having achieved
some order and direction in our fragmented and disordered lives
that we cannot imagine wanting anything beyond that—but in
time we may be afflicted with *accidia*, traditionally called
"sloth" but better understood as a boredom or apathy that leads
to despair. Evagrius refers to it as the "noonday demon," in an
allusion to Psalm 91:6 and "the destruction that wastes at
noonday." Apparently boredom afflicted the monks particularly
at noontime devotions, just as today our minds can wander
during sermons or long prayers in church.

More generally, despair arises from discouragement over our
lack of personal progress in the Christian life, the failures of
fellow Christians, meanspiritedness and gossip, and church
politics. Love between Christians is not in evidence: no one
seems genuinely interested in anyone else. In short, despair is
what tells us that we do not seem to be getting anywhere in the
spiritual life, and the church as a whole does not seem to be
making any progress either.

Julian of Norwich, the fourteenth-century English mystic,
confessed that she was afflicted with despair for many years

before the revelations or "showings" of Christ's sufferings restored her hope. She came to realize, as John Bunyan did later
in *Pilgrim's Progress*, that such discouragement is part of the
spiritual journey and not a sign that we have departed from the
path.

As serious as despair is—Evagrius says that of all the deadly
thoughts it causes the monastic the most trouble of all—it
should not be confused with a far more advanced spiritual
condition known as "the dark night of the soul." This phrase
was made famous by John of the Cross in his treatise *Ascent to
Mt. Carmel* and it has become part of the common vocabulary
of spiritual theology. Unfortunately, people who do not know
the work of John of the Cross frequently trivialize the term by
applying it indiscriminately to any emotional distress or temptation to lose faith, rather than to a specific spiritual condition.
Even a slight familiarity with the writings of John of the Cross
makes clear that very few people enter the spiritual path he
describes—one of utter abandonment of all possessions, and all
self-direction. During this journey one experiences several kinds
of "dark nights" (of the senses, emotions, and thought), losing
in each all contact with God. What is experienced by many
people who use the expression "dark night of the soul" is more
likely to be garden-variety boredom or despair. This kind of
spiritual depression is serious and must be combated, while the
dark night of the soul is positive, as it purifies. Spiritual depression occurs because we have not yet achieved sufficient inte-
gration and harmony; it is part of the active life. The dark night
of the soul occurs in those who have achieved an integrated
spirituality and a purity of heart that powerfully draws them
toward God as their treasure. It is belongs to the contemplative,
rather than the active, life.

Of course, we can also expect to make progress in the
spiritual life, and when we do, we risk going to the opposite
extreme of discouragement, which is vainglory, the seventh
deadly thought. As we find ourselves improving in obedience,
we want others to notice it. We try to make our loyalty to God
known publicly. Remember Christ's warning about those who
stand in the marketplace to pray, and who make sure that

everyone knows how much money they contribute to the Temple (Matt. 6:1-6)? We may in all innocence continue to praise God for enabling us to progress spiritually, as people frequently do at testimonial meetings, punctuated by "Praise the Lord!", but it is clear that we suffer from vainglory when we start to think we are superior to others, like the Pharisee who went up in the Temple to pray (Luke 18:10-14). When we are assailed by vainglory we long for praise and for prestige; we are annoyed and even depressed when we do not get the recognition we think we deserve. Envy of others is also a common expression of vainglory.

Samuel Johnson, who composed the first dictionary in English, once spoke of fame as the vain desire to fill the mind of others with yourself. This desire is hopeless because, however large a place you occupy in the minds of others, it is tiny compared to the place they themselves occupy there. It is also terribly difficult to maintain a place in other people's minds for long: there are so many competitors for their attention. It is a vain or hopeless desire.

Evagrius points out that those who are afflicted with vainglory quite often succumb to lust, one of the most elementary sins. This suggests that someone who has made great progress and becomes overly pleased by it is able to be humiliated by what was supposed to have long ago been conquered. Perhaps it is not accidental that public figures who are greatly admired can be guilty of serious sexual impropriety. At any rate, it is important for those who have made progress in following Christ to remember that they are branches and Christ is the true vine. The good fruit they bear is because of Christ's life at work in them, and without Christ they are vulnerable to the very temptations to which they thought they had long ago become immune.

Frequently vainglory is accompanied by pride, the eighth deadly thought. With vainglory, we crave notice of our achievements; with pride, we take full credit for the progress we have made and do not think that God has been involved at all, let alone been our indispensable helper. This leads to a sense of superiority. As Evagrius puts it, "He gets a big head in regard to the brethren, considering them stupid because they do not all have this same opinion of him."[6] Anger and sadness follow on the heels of pride precisely because others do not share our high opinion of ourselves. Evagrius also points out that pride can even lead to mental derangement; in its milder forms, it encourages a distorted view of ourselves, our neighbor, and God.

Our inherent sense of self-worth and our desire for self-realization are God-given. The capacity to respond to God's intentions, actively seeking to realize the potential God has bestowed on us, gives us dignity. God also respects our integrity by seeking to give us the fullness we seek with our participation; he does not exercise sheer power on us, and so we can always refuse. Yet God continues to call us to respond, seeking to restore us to the path that leads to genuine self-realization. The crux is whether we believe that God seeks our fulfillment, and that God's way is the way to our fulfillment. If we do not perceive that God's goodness, justice, and love include a desire for our well-being, then we see only God's power and find hateful the idea of any dependence on God.

The Christian vocabulary of self-renunciation, rejection of pride, and obedience violently clashes with contemporary culture, which values self-affirmation, self-realization, self-esteem, and empowerment. It is certainly correct for us to turn away from self-rejection, which is a very powerful tendency within us, but to understand the Christian language of self-renunciation we need to understand the role of social prestige in the way we evaluate ourselves and our worth. Although we want to think well of ourselves, we cannot love ourselves *directly* and this leads us to desire, admire, seek, or love what has social prestige and value and to identify ourselves with it. Then we can think well of ourselves. We are proud to be members of an excellent football team or a respected profession, or to work for a major company. We bask in the reflected glory of something society esteems, and it gives us self-esteem and energy.

According to Christian teachings, if our self-understanding and self-evaluation arise wholly from our social position, then we cannot receive them from God. Whether we have a high or low self-evaluation, we cannot perceive the potential God has in store for us. That is why God's call to liberation, to freedom from this distorted view of ourselves, is heard as a call to self-destruction. The call to reject pride, to become humble, and to make sacrifices sounds oppressive, beside the point, and clearly not the way to live happily.

Ironically, it is the very urge to live well, which God has given us, that drives us to seek fullness elsewhere and resist God's call. The need to think well of ourselves is something that both leads us to God and blocks us from God. The human condition is such that God's call is always initially heard in a distorted form. Until we can hear more clearly, with some detachment, God seems the enemy of our self-realization.

The opposite of pride is humility. Humility does not mean that we lie about our talents and achievements, but that we realize that all of us are equally creatures, and that nothing we have or can do raises us above that status. We find our identity in attending to God, and receiving from God the power to love others. The need to think well of ourselves, which is the very thing that leads to idolatry, disorder, and self-hatred, is the same need that leads to love of God, to love of neighbor, to community, and to peace, within and without. Like all the other deadly vices, pride too is the perversion of a God-given need and desire. The traditional prayer book collect makes perfect sense when it instructs us to pray to the One "in whose service is perfect freedom."

Evagrius claims that the eight deadly thoughts agitate us, causing us to experience disordered passions. Passion comes from *passive;* it is to be acted upon by something. The passions that the eight deadly thoughts arouse inhibit the work of the Holy Spirit in our lives and keep us from loving God and our neighbor. In the next chapter we will look at some of the classic remedies for the eight deadly thoughts.

Notes

1. Maximus the Confessor, *Four Hundred Chapters on Love*, George C. Berthold, trans. (Mahwah, N. J.: Paulist Press, 1985), 2.38.

2. Two valuable sources are *The God of Thinness: Gluttony and Other Weighty Matters* by Mary Louise Bringle, and "Gluttony: Thought for Food," an unpublished article by Dennis Olkham in which he draws upon the entire ascetical tradition to deal with our present-day problems with food.

3. Maximus, *Four Hundred Chapters*, 2.39.

4. Owen Chadwick, *John Cassian*, 2nd edition (Cambridge: Cambridge University Press, 1968), 94.

5. John Calvin, *Institutes*, 3.10.2-3.

6. Evagrius, *Praktikos*, ch. 14.

CHAPTER SIX

PROGRESS IN THE SPIRITUAL LIFE

After conversion, the goal for every Christian is *apatheia*. It is a word made famous by Stoicism and means freedom from the inner turbulence caused by the eight deadly thoughts. *Apatheia* is not to be confused with apathy or lack of feeling; in fact, lack of feeling is equal to boredom and despair, where we are unmoved by love of Christian teachings and worship. By contrast, to achieve Christian *apatheia* means we have progressed so far in the Christian life that these appetites and our thoughts about them do not continually agitate and disturb us. Christians who are free of the burden of the eight deadly thoughts are better able to love their neighbor and to improve in love and knowledge of God. Far from being unfeeling or unmoved, they are powerfully moved by Christ's love, by the beauty of God's creation, by acts of kindness and justice, and by the hope of the life to come. St. Jerome completely misunderstood the desert monastics in regard to *apatheia* when he accused them of seeking to become like a stone; he confused the Christian and Stoic understandings of the word.

Christians seek to be free of the turmoil caused by uncontrolled passions primarily in order to obey God. That is why we understand *apatheia* as a purity of heart that allows us to love our neighbor and frees us to contemplate and pray without undue distraction. Evagrius called *apatheia* "the very flower of ascesis."[1] Rather than seeking to be independent of everything, like the Stoic, the Christian seeks to become wholly dependent on God's love and more deeply involved with the well-being of others.

The Greek word *monachos* (monk), which was used to describe the desert monastics, was also used to mean "single" or "undivided." The *monachos* has interior unity or purity of heart, bringing the whole self to focus on God and to desire God as the sole treasure. Unless we can bring our scattered thoughts and feelings into focus, we cannot see or understand ourselves, our neighbor, or the created universe, nor can we proceed from this indirect knowledge to direct knowledge of God face-to-face. Perhaps an analogy will help.

The eye condition known as astigmatism prevents the light rays that the eye admits from being focused and as a result the sufferer cannot see clearly. However, a corrective lens can focus the light correctly and ensure proper vision. Similarly, ascetical practices such as prayer, fasting, reading, and almsgiving help us to gain sufficient mastery over ourselves so that we can bring our entire self into focus. As long as our attention is distracted because we ourselves are divided in our wishes, wants, desires, and hopes, we cannot attend to the word of God. Without such contact, we cannot be purified over time and made whole. Purity of heart is the acquired ability to gather more and more of our scattered desires into focus as we come more and more to desire the good that God seeks to give us: holiness, love, peace, joy, discernment, and full union with God. The beatitude "Blessed are the pure in heart, for they shall see God" was a favorite monastic text.

Another way to understand that the detachment of ascetical theology is a rejection of the turbulence stirred up by the eight deadly thoughts, not a rejection of feeling, is the image of "the wound of knowledge." The Christian is not invulnerable. As Julian of Norwich wrote in her *Showings*, the Christian life requires three wounds: the wound of repentance, the wound of compassion, and the wound of longing for the love of God. These wounds should not be avoided because there is no knowledge possible of ourselves, of others, and of God that is invulnerable or unfeeling.

⌇ ⌇

What remedies does spiritual theology recommend for the eight deadly thoughts if we are to progress on the path that leads to God? Some remedies that Evagrius recommends are reading, vigils, and prayer; these "lend stability to the wandering mind"[2] and help overcome fragmentation and division within. By reading he means primarily *lectio divina*, "reading divine things," a prayerful reading of the Bible, commentary on scripture, or theological writings. We will consider this later, but here we can say in general that to focus our attention on "divine things" makes us more like God.

In ascetical theology this principle springs not only from the Bible but from actual human experience. Attention to what is good and holy does in fact have the capacity to turn our minds from dwelling on ourselves and to lessen our anger and pride. Maximus the Confessor points out that "the praiseworthy passion of love binds [the mind] even to divine things. For generally where the mind devotes its time it also expands, and where it expands it also turns its desire and love."[3] In own time Simone Weil claimed, "Attention is the only faculty of the soul that gives us access to God." One of the most common phrases in the Rule of St. Benedict is "Listen, my son," while we find in the Old Testament and in Jewish piety the constant refrain "Hear, O Israel."

Vigils are one form of paying attention. They usually are held in a holy place where we focus our mind on some holy event, such as the birth of Christ, his temptations in the wilderness, his transfiguration, or his crucifixion, and engage in meditation, prayer, and self-examination. The practice of vigils or waiting in a holy place with our attention on some holy event or events has the effect of renewing our focus on Christ in the face of many competing desires that pull us in different directions.

Evagrius also mentions that "hunger, toil and solitude are the means of extinguishing the flames of desire."[4] He is referring to the hunger of fasting, the constant reminder of the sacrifices made for us by God incarnate in his earthly life. Each time we feel hunger or resist the temptation to eat and drink we are reminded of why we are not eating or drinking, namely because we want to become people whose entire heart, mind, soul, and strength are devoted to loving God. We can also give our surplus to others who are in need and learn to use the things of this world properly. Should we be attracted to fasting for less worthwhile reasons, such as losing weight for cosmetic reasons, these very thoughts help us recognize the mixed nature of our motives.

The expression "habitual reminders" is a part of the vocabulary of spiritual theology and means the practice of calling God habitually to mind. The phylacteries, small receptacles bound to the forehead and arm by Jews at prayer, remind them of God, as do religious festivals such as Passover, Temple worship, and grace before meals. In the gospels, Jesus commanded that the Last Supper be observed as a reminder of his death until he returned. The basic psychological fact here is that just as we are taught to brush our teeth regularly after meals until it becomes second nature, so too habitual reminders accustom us to live more and more in God's presence.

One of the most important barriers to the spiritual life is that we tend to regard God as our opponent, not our helper. This is understandable. As we make progress in the spiritual life and become more aware of our inadequacies, we fear that God will make us give up doing something we want to do or make us do something we do not want to do. But God *imposes* nothing on us. To those who have come to dwell in God, God is patient and kind. If we continue to open ourselves to God, sooner or later we will find that things we once did we now gladly relinquish, and that many things we once feared to do we now do gladly. This is because God quietly dwells within us, often without our awareness. Now and again we become surprised by our obedience. Sometimes it is best to ignore for a while the things that most trouble our consciences and to attend to God as we are, leaving it to God to deal with the situation and trusting that the habits of regular reading, vigils, fasting, observances, and the like will have their positive effect in time.

Evagrius also mentions the spiritual value of physical work, the most common kind of work done by the desert monastics. Fatigue has a way of defusing our passions and reminding us of our mortality. Work is also a reminder that God too works as creator, sustainer, and redeemer, and invites us, just as he invited Adam and Eve, to join him in the care of the universe. In recommending physical toil, we see once again that the desert monastics, rather than having scorn for the body, saw bodily work as having spiritual value. The Protestant reformers went even further by stressing the spiritual value of all forms of constructive work, an attitude captured in George Herbert's poem "The Elixir," which later became a famous hymn.

Teach me, my God and King,
In all things thee to see,
And what I do in anything,
To do it as for thee:

Not rudely, as a beast,
To run into an action;
But still to make thee prepossest,
And give it his perfection.

A man that looks on glass,
On it may stay his eye;
Or if he pleaseth, through it pass,
And then the heav'n espy.

All may of thee partake:
Nothing can be so mean,
Which with this tincture (for thy sake)
Will not grow bright and clean.

A servant with this clause
Makes drudgery divine:

Who sweeps a room, as for thy laws,
Makes that and th' action fine.

This is the famous stone
That turneth all to gold:
For that which God doth touch and own
Cannot for less be told.

Herbert's line "not rudely, as a beast, to run into an action" suggests an important mark of spiritual maturity. To perform actions "rudely" is to act without knowing the reason for the action. Even religious beliefs and practices can be performed "rudely"—automatically. Perhaps they are done out of conformity to the religious, political, or social actions and beliefs of our parents and never become fully our own. In that case we lack sufficient self-direction; we do not have insight into the point of a practice, or the meaning and grounds for a belief. Consequently we follow a practice or hold to a belief inflexibly, making no allowances for the fact that a particular practice may not be appropriate for a particular situation. That is why some of the scribes and Pharisees attacked Jesus for some of his teachings and actions, such as healing a man on the sabbath. Jesus did not deny the importance of observance of the sabbath, but he pointed out that to heal on the sabbath did not violate it, since the sabbath was made for the benefit of people, not people for the sabbath (Mark 2:27–3:5). To cast off the practices and beliefs with which we were raised is not in itself a sign of maturity. This rejection may be part of an adolescent rebellion rather than a new insight or a deeper understanding of the gospel. Herbert's opening words, "Teach me, my God and King," strike the right note: if we are to grow spiritually, understanding must accompany our piety.

Evagrius also mentions solitude as a valuable remedy. Many of us fear being alone, but solitude is not isolation. It is an opportunity to grow in dependence on God, and so to gain some detachment from prevailing social norms. Solitude gives us the opportunity for undivided attention. To experience solitude requires us to be alone, but in being alone we can experience the presence of Christian community through the ages—the communion of saints—as we read scripture, pray, and fast. It is a rich and uplifting experience to know such solitude. It is not isolation because we are part of a larger community that belongs to Christ, the head of the church, and in all our actions, even when alone, we join others in seeking God's kingdom. Isolation is one of the painful consequences of sin; solitude destroys isolation.

There is one remedy I have found very helpful for the destructive passion of anger. This is particularly important to me because for years I have suffered from a short fuse and inordinate anger. I have been able to recognize that some of my anger is the result of frustration: often I believe I know the best way to get things done but my seminary colleagues prevent what is "best" from happening. All too frequently, as we go through the procedures of new appointments or promotions, discuss curricular reforms, and the like, I find myself increasingly agitated by the obstructive tactics used again and again by people who, I think, should know better. Then I begin to see them as my enemies.

The frustration I suffer is one that Dante attributed to Satan in the last circle of hell. Satan's rage at God's way of arranging things causes him to keep flapping his wings, generating icy gusts that cause the lake to remain frozen and Satan himself to be locked in impotence. This insight into anger helped me some. So too did psychological accounts of the causes and remedies for anger that I read. But it was not such understanding that relieved me of the burden of intemperate anger. To my surprise, I found in the ancient practice of *lectio divina* immense relief from evil thoughts and the agitation they produce.

Lectio divina consists of four interlocking parts: reading a passage of scripture to yourself aloud; meditating or thinking about what you have read; praying about what has risen up in your mind and heart in meditation; and then contemplation—simply resting silently in God for a time after you have prayed. It is vitally important to read the scriptures aloud. We have become so skillful at reading rapidly that our eyes just race down the page. Not only does reading aloud help us slow down, but hearing the words uttered aloud helps us take in what we read much better.

When I was introduced to this method, I was given Psalm 139 to read. I was struck by this passage:

> They talk blasphemously about you,
>   regard your thoughts as nothing.
> Yahweh, do I not hate those who hate you,
>   and loathe those who defy you?
> I hate them with a total hatred,
>   I regard them as my own enemies. (Ps. 139:20-22, NIV)

As I repeated these verses to myself, I began to think about the theological seminary where I teach and what is said about God in courses and books by the theologians I knew and those I came across at academic meetings. All too often, it seemed to me, my fellow theologians "blasphemed" and "regarded as nothing" God's thoughts as revealed in scripture. I realized that I did hate them, and believed my anger and hatred well-founded. Suddenly it occurred to me that perhaps *God* did not regard them as his enemies, even though I did. My mind and heart began to be stretched by this possibility. If God did not regard them as his enemies, then they could not be my enemies either.

This meditation led me immediately into prayer, as it is supposed to do in *lectio*. In prayer I confessed that I had acted presumptuously in condemning others as God's enemies, and had become self-righteous in scorning them. I asked to be forgiven and to be helped in no longer regarding them as my enemies. A few hours later I found myself with a deep sense of peace, and not long after that a joyful spirit kept bubbling up unbidden. I had not yet been taught that this practice often leads to the experience of deep peace and joy. I am glad that I had not been told this ahead of time, as I might have suspected that mere psychological suggestion had led to these feelings.

I now find that when I am irritated or angry with others I can often calm my agitation with the reminder, "They are not my enemies." Sometimes I hum or sing to myself part of a psalm, as Evagrius recommends. The results astound me: I think I am finally becoming free of the tyranny of inordinate and senseless anger. Although I am still deeply concerned with what is taught and written about God, when I criticize people's work I no longer do it with as much bitterness and scorn as I once did—and what I say is now taken with more seriousness than before.

The peace and joy that arise from this practice come from the presence of God the Holy Spirit. Its tranquility can be compared to the harmonizing notes of the bass clef that are sounded more or less continuously beneath a melody in the treble clef. God's peace and joy (bass clef) can thus coexist with many other thoughts and feelings (treble clef), and God's peace and joy can be brought to awareness by a simple shift of attention. This is one way we may have a *habitual* awareness of God. It was my hunger for habitual presence that led me to the study of spirituality in the first place.

The practices of the desert monastics are not necessarily to be followed just as they stand in written texts. On the basis of his own and other people's experience Evagrius himself points out that the practices he recommends "are to be engaged in according to due measure and at the appropriate time." Here he is alluding to the need for a spiritual director or guide so that people will not overdo the remedies of fasting or reading or prayer, or do them at inappropriate times in light of their responsibilities.

He also points out that we can overreach ourselves and, when we do, we are unable to sustain what we have undertaken. This can lead to a terrible, destructive reaction. As Jesus pointed out in a parable, when the Holy Spirit does not enter the place that was previously occupied by a demon that has been cast out, seven demons rush in and leave the person worse off than before. Therefore, Evagrius cautions, "What is untimely done, or done without measure, endures but a short time. And what is short lived is more harmful than profitable."[5]

In writing about the freedom of the Christian, Martin Luther captured the purpose of the desert monastics with his remark, "A Christian is a perfectly free lord of all, subject to none. A Christian is a perfectly dutiful servant of all, subject to all."[6] Both the desert monastics and the reformers share the conviction that, through the Spirit, Christ has united himself to us, and that progress in the Christian spiritual journey is the increase of that unity. The effort to overcome the eight deadly thoughts is to allow Christ, not our passions, to control us. The desert monastics sought to become free of the various passions that hinder or block God's love from flowing into us and out of us. We may capture their view by a comparison with the way a well can be kept from going dry. As long as water is drawn from a well, underground rivulets can replenish it. But if a well is not used, in time the tiny channels become full of pebbles, sand, and silt, until eventually the well becomes dry.

꒦ ꒦

The charge that Christian spirituality is too concerned with the inner life and thus makes people self-absorbed, therefore, is not necessarily true. Spirituality is social, and many of the eight deadly thoughts are social, arising from comparing ourselves to others (sadness), from injury (anger at others), and from the desire that others praise us (vainglory). When we seek to abide in Christ, in wrestling with those things that hinder this union we increasingly find our identity in Christ rather than in the values and constructs of the communities in which we live.

Over the course of our spiritual journey, our motives for undertaking it become increasingly pure. In his eleventh *Conference* Cassian recognizes that many of us are initially moved by a fear of hell and think of God solely in terms of his power. Such a fear is called *attrition*. Attrition is spiritually sterile—unlike *contrition*, where our fear stems from our belief in God's justice and is accompanied by a hope for mercy and forgiveness. The fear of hell haunted Luther before he discovered justification by faith, and his fear greatly hindered his reception of God's love. As we progress in our journey, we may obey God increasingly out of attraction rather than fear: the ability to control our appetites for food, sexual pleasure, material goods; freedom from self-destructive anger, and the like. We also grow in gratitude for his forgiveness. As Maximus the Confessor wrote,

The one who fears the Lord always has humility as his companion and through its promptings is led to divine love and thanksgiving....With fear he receives love as well, ever thankful with deep humility to the benefactor and pilot of our life.[7]

Simone Weil believed that we are delivered from evil only through contact with divine purity, since contact with anything that is less than pure cannot relieve us of evil. It is not absorbed, but is returned to us. Yet "if through attention and desire we put a part of our evil onto something perfectly pure, it cannot soil it; it remains pure; it does not return the evil; thus we are delivered from it."[8] Weil mentions some of the things "here below" that are perfectly pure, such as the beauty of nature or of religious texts and objects. All of them draw their purity from God, and because they do, we may be delivered from the burden of evil by our attention to them.

In Psalm 112 we find the same progression from obedience because of fear to obedience because of our love of God for his benefits.

> Happy are those who fear the Lord,
>   who greatly delight in his commandments.
> Their descendants will be mighty in the land....
> Wealth and riches are in their houses. (Ps. 112:1-3)

The psalm culminates, however, in our generosity to others because of what we have received:

> They have distributed freely,
>   they have given to the poor. (vs. 9)

This is precisely the progression described in ascetical theology: the practice of discipline, begun in fear and continued in gratitude for its benefits, culminates in love of neighbor.

Beyond both fear and reward there is love for God himself. As we find ourselves acting out of love for God, we are moved by a new kind of fear. Owen Chadwick describes it as the fear by which children honor their parents, and spouses and friends honor one another: "Not a fear of blows or quarrel, but of some flaw in love."[9] Few things in life make us more miserable than to fail those who love us and have made great sacrifices for us. How much more may we be grieved by our failure to follow Christ.

In George Herbert's long poem sequence *The Temple* we see a similar progression from fear of punishment to love. The parameters of the Christian pilgrimage he describes are a stone heart, which he calls the altar, and God's love which, being refused, results in the sacrifice of Christ. The movement of the pilgrimage is the transformation of stony hearts into hearts that yield to God's love. This contrast between fear of punishment and love is briefly stated in these lines from the poem "Discipline":

> Then let wrath remove;
> Love will do the deed:
>   For with love
> Stony hearts will bleed. (17-20)

The movement to be traced is one that begins with the perception of God's wrath and moves to the perception of God's love, which can move stony hearts to weep for the grief they have caused. For Herbert the primary question of the Christian life is what we can render to God in the face of Christ's sacrifice for us.

The longest poem in *The Temple* is entitled "The Sacrifice." Each stanza but the last ends with the question "Was ever grief like mine?" Christ himself is the speaker throughout the poem; he describes the love which seeks us and the grief our lack of response causes him. Herbert's point in "The Sacrifice" is that we cannot defeat God's love and design; our rejection is turned into a sacrifice. For instead of rejecting us for our rejection, God takes our very rejection and turns it into a revelation. It reveals the magnitude of God's love; of God's willingness to put up with our blindness, our folly, our evil. God's response to all that we are and have done is not rejection, but painful endurance. God lets us see the effects of all that we have done by letting our actions destroy Christ's body, but God also shows us that God's love cannot be turned away. Even when people killed the one who bears the love of God, God raised Christ from the dead to claim us. The greatest rejection of all is not able to defeat God's love. We are to see in the suffering our rejection causes a precise measure and revelation of the extent and tenacity of his love. Our rejection becomes the very truth that he cares for us: "I, who am Truth, turn into truth their deeds."

It is the perception of the grief we have caused and the desire to respond adequately that gives the motivation and the goal of the pilgrimage: a stony heart changed into an fit altar, a dwelling place of divine love, as Herbert notes in "The Altar":

A heart alone
Is such a stone,
As nothing but
Thy pow'r doth cut....
O let thy blessed sacrifice be mine,
And sanctify this altar to be thine.

We do not learn until the end of The Temple, in the poem "Love," and, indeed not until the last line of that poem, what the proper response to the sacrifice of Christ is. We learn at the table of the eucharist that finally all that we can do and are asked to do is to receive his sacrificial love for us: to rejoice with love in his love.

And know you not, says Love, who bore the blame?
    My dear, then I will serve.
You must sit down, says Love, and taste my meat:
    So I did sit and eat.

∾   ∾

If we feel that we have not progressed very far in the spiritual journey, perhaps we have not wrestled seriously enough with what hinders us from experiencing Christ's presence more fully. When some monks visited Maximus the Confessor and complained that because they did not find themselves full of love Christ must have abandoned them, Maximus told them that they had simply grown careless. The treasures that are Christ's were not shown forth in their lives because they had become lax in following his commandments. How could Christ reveal himself in their lives when they failed to make a consistent effort to follow his ways? Peace, joy, generosity, understanding of life, and wisdom are gifts, but to receive them requires our earnest efforts. "This is the treasure hidden in the field of your heart," he rebukes them, "which you have not yet found because of laziness, for if you had found it you would then have sold everything to acquire that field. But now you abandon the field and give your attention to nearby things, in which you find nothing but thorns and burrs."[10] It is not accidental that the Bible contains so many passages telling us to wake up and be attentive, such as, "Sleeper, awake! Rise from the dead, and Christ will shine on you" (Eph. 5:14).

Perhaps what hinders many of us in our spiritual journey is not so much carelessness, but our tendency to judge the gospel strictly in terms of punishment and hope of reward. Many of us pay attention only to those aspects of the gospel. George Gallup reports that the reason most people in America cease to go to church is that they or someone they love has undergone some hardship, such as a financial reversal or illness. They are like the plant in the parable of the sower, which sprang up quickly but wilted under the heat of the sun because it was in shallow soil and lacked deep roots.

Another indication of progress is the development of integrity and discernment. In ascetical theology, integrity, or wholeness, refers to control of the passions. A human nature restored to the condition God originally intended is harmonious. Our appetites for food, drink, sexual pleasure, material goods, and the like do not disappear, but they are properly expressed. We never reach the point where we are utterly free of the eight deadly thoughts, but we do make progress. Maximus makes an important distinction when he reminds us, "It is one thing to sin from habit and other to sin by being carried away."[11] As we progress in the faith and our character is reshaped, we tend to become more integrated or whole persons, disposed toward goodness. When we sin, it is usually an impulsive act, rather than premeditated and deliberate. We also recognize our fault more easily, and repent of it more promptly. When the desert monastics speak of the purity needed for contemplation of God, they do not mean that we never sin. Rather, they mean that we have a new disposition or tendency to move beyond fear of punishment and desire for reward to a love of God for God's own self.

Discernment is the ability to assess our spiritual condition. Part of the difficulty is knowing on what basis we are to make an evaluation; even with the guidance of the threefold way, the eight deadly thoughts, and the indications of spiritual progress we have mentioned so far, we still need skill in using these and other standards. It is hard enough to make sound judgments in mundane matters, much less in matters of the spirit. We often think that our only problem is doing what is good and refraining from evil, and we assume it is not difficult to tell good from evil. Those who are spiritually mature know that this is frequently not the case; they know how often they have been fooled into thinking that something is good, realizing only when well into its pursuit that it is not. Similarly, it is easy to find an important discipline or practice oppressive at first, only to realize later that it really is good for us. Only by practice and after repeated mistakes—which take courage to admit—do we develop discernment, if we develop it at all.

The Protestant reformers rejected the notion of a neat, direct, orderly progression in the spiritual life. Luther in particular was so opposed to the notion of "stages" that he frequently appears to reject any notion of sanctification. He was fearful of relying on subjective states of feeling as an indication of where we stand in relation to God. Yet the fear that self-reliance or works righteousness is inherent to growth in Christian maturity is easily dispelled by looking again at one remedy for temptation that was taught to the desert hermits, as reported by Abbot Isaac to John Cassian:

> For keeping up continual recollection of God, this pious formula is to be ever set before you: "O God, make speed to save me: O Lord, make haste to help me." (Ps. 70:1)

Abbot Isaac goes on to point out the virtues of this prayer:

> It contains an invocation of God against every danger, it contains humble and pious confession, it contains the watchfulness of anxiety and continual fear, it contains the thought of one's own weakness, confidence in the answer, and the assurance of a present and ready help.[12]

Notes

1. Evagrius, *Praktikos*, 81.

2. *Ibid.*, 15.

3. Maximus the Confessor, *Four Centuries*, 3.72. Aristotle's theory of knowledge is based on the idea that we become what we know. This idea was employed by Plotinus in his account of the spiritual ascent of the soul to the One, and had some influence on medieval spirituality.

4. Evagrius, *Praktikos*, 20.

5. *Ibid.*, 15.

6. Martin Luther, "The Freedom of a Christian" in *Works*, Jarislov Pelikan, ed. (St. Louis: Concordia Publishing House, 1955-86), 21:344.

7. Maximus, *Four Centuries*, 1.48.

8. Simone Weil, *Pensees sans ordre concernant l'amour de Dieu* (Paris: Galimard, 1962), 15. My translation.

9. Owen Chadwick, *John Cassian*, 2nd edition (Cambridge: Cambridge University Press, 1968), 101. Maximus makes a similar distinction between two kinds of fear in *Four Centuries*, 1:81-82.

10. Maximus, *Four Centuries*, 4.71.

11. *Ibid.*, 3.71.

12. John Cassian, *Conferences*, in *Nicene and Post-Nicene Fathers*, 2nd series, Philip Schaff and Henry Wace, eds. (Grand Rapids: Eerdmans, 1955), 11:405.

CHAPTER SEVEN

CONTEMPLATION

Spiritual theology has two aspects, the active and the contemplative. Yet we have already seen that the active life, which is concerned with the goals of ascetical theology, such as overcoming the passions and loving our neighbor, also teaches meditative and contemplative practices (vigils, prayers, and *lectio divina*) that help us act lovingly toward all people. So there is not an absolute contrast between the active and the contemplative life. In both there are meditative and contemplative practices; the differences lie in the goal toward which each is directed.

Maximus the Confessor points out that in the active life the focus of our attention is obedience to Christ's teachings and overcoming the hindrances to our obedience. In the contemplative life, however, the focus of our attention is doctrines, which enlighten the mind and give us knowledge of God:

> By means of the commandments the Lord renders detached those who carry them out; by means of the divine doctrines he bestows on them the enlightenment of knowledge.[1]

In the active life we become like God by acting like God—we become generous, for example, by acting with generosity. In the contemplative life, we become like God through knowing God's wisdom, which increases our love for God and in turn our love for our neighbor.

Sometimes the terms meditation and contemplation are used interchangeably in the tradition; sometimes the latter is reserved for wordless, imageless attentiveness, as we will see when we examine the mystical fourteenth-century work, *The Cloud of Unknowing*. In this chapter I will use the terms contemplation and meditation interchangeably to mean a focused, directed state of prayer.

Although there are many practices and writings on Christian meditation and contemplation, most Christians do not know what they are supposed to do when they meditate or contemplate. Until recently the only practices with which they were familiar were spoken prayers and daily devotions, but as techniques of eastern meditation have been introduced into the West the word "meditation" has become well-known to church people and secularists alike. However, the kind of meditation and contemplation that I intend is different: it is primarily the Bible that one is to read and think about in meditation, and it is in God's arms that one is to rest in contemplation.

The contemplative life we are going to examine in the rest of this book requires rational thinking, and its motivation is to increase our love for our neighbor and our love for God. The content of our meditation is supplied by the two "books" of God, nature and scripture. Contemplation, in which we rest in God, takes place *after* we have actively meditated on the things of God.

I vividly recall my first serious experience in the practice of meditation and contemplation. It was during an eight-day retreat for training spiritual directors and we were sitting quietly in the chapel after a service of worship. After ten or fifteen minutes of silence I began to think that this was all very well, but I had an awful lot of important matters waiting to be done, including some theological research and writing. Then it suddenly struck me how much of my religious life had been centered on reading and writing about God, while very little of it had been spent waiting silently in God's presence, and virtually none waiting silently with other people. Gradually I came to realize that I was not wasting time, even though for the moment other things were not getting done. I slowly realized that I had not made enough time in this particular way for God in my life; I was far too burdened with what I thought I had to do, and not nearly open enough to receiving God's help and strength in doing various needful things. As I gradually released the thought that I was wasting time, I began to recognize that as we sat there together silently, we were in contact with God and each other, and that together we were receiving God the Holy Spirit into our lives.

Quakers, of course, have known the value of corporate silence from the time of their founding, but I think my initial reaction to sitting quietly for a substantial period as a waste of time is probably typical of most people in our society today, including most church people. We do not regard it as a way to knowledge of God and, through knowledge of God, to growth in love for God and for our neighbor. Many of us simply do not sit still for significant periods of time, and even should we think that it is good for us to do so, we do not know what we should be thinking about in order to meditate or contemplate.

The widespread notion that contemplation is a waste of time arises in part from the notion that spirituality is concerned only with individual piety. Spirituality is thought to neglect our relation to larger communities and, in its preference for contemplation, to neglect action in the wider world. Yet the active and contemplative life, symbolized by Mary and Martha, were understood in the early church as two functions that are part of every Christian's life. Contemplation is not restricted to monastics, nor can it be said to lead to the heresy of quietism—utter passivity—when the Society of Friends has been famous for its social activism throughout its history. Even if there were a tendency for those who are attracted to contemplation to take less part in social action, why should those who are not very interested in contemplation hold up their own way of following Christ as superior to all others? Is that any different from arguing that monasticism is the best way of being a Christian?

My own view is that action and reflection are on a continuum, with different Christian communities and individuals existing at different points on the continuum, and all Christians are to exhibit some of each in their lives. All practicing Christians are involved to various degrees with prayer, the Bible, the beauty of the world, and a belief in God's providence—and all of these are the very substance of contemplation.

My approach to the massively rich and diverse material on prayer, meditation, and contemplation will be primarily to specify what we are to think about when we meditate or contemplate. Although I will draw on various types of prayer and accounts of meditation, I will not give a survey of the many kinds of prayer nor examine different types of meditation and contemplation by various spiritual teachers. Instead, I will concentrate on the main purpose of the contemplative life, which is to perceive all things in relation to God and to know God's continuous presence in and through them.

ஃ ஃ

In the 1950s Iris Murdoch, then an Oxford philosopher and soon-to-be major novelist, became concerned over the decline of conscience—which she defined as personal inner dialogue, the meditation on a person or situation—as a major part of our ethical and spiritual lives. One of the reasons for the demise of the importance of conscience in ethical theory lies in the fact that conscience was put forward in the eighteenth century as an infallible guide to right and wrong, good and evil. The view of conscience that Murdoch advanced, however, was different: for her, conscience is the inner dialogue of mind and heart through which we try to discern whether we are judging people and situations with justice.

One example she gives is the mother-in-law who feels that her son has married beneath him, but in time comes to wonder if she is really being fair. Is her daughter-in-law really vulgar and talkative, or simply unaffected and high-spirited? With this and other examples Murdoch shows that we have to consider and reconsider our judgments of other people and situations because we suffer from a built-in distortion that corrupts our judgments. We see all things from our own point of view, and with an enormously inflated sense of self-importance, which does not allow us to recognize the reality of others. Through conscience we seek to correct our distorted vision and perceive more accurately what is before us.

For Murdoch, therefore, ethics is an activity taking place in every moment of time; all that we do, think, and feel affects the kind of person we become, either moving us nearer to a more just vision of the people and situations we encounter each day, or confirming us in our self-enclosed outlook. (For most people movement can happen in either direction at any time). All our activities and thoughts have relevance because they can help us, bit by bit, to become more free of distorted perceptions.

This internal dialogue may take place in the most unpromising places and circumstances, as Murdoch illustrates in her novel *Bruno's Dream*. An old man, now bedridden, is slowly dying of old age. Never very successful either in his work or as a husband and parent, his only notable achievements are his love and knowledge of spiders and his affection for the stamps in a valuable stamp collection he has inherited. Now that he is old and dying, he is even more marginal, having little effect on the events of his world.

Yet the novel suggests that a morally significant activity is taking place as his body slowly undergoes biological decay. For Bruno is deep in an internal conversation, recalling the "dream" that was his life, especially his unsatisfactory relationship with his dead wife. What had gone wrong? What had she wanted to tell him at the end when she called to him so frantically and he avoided coming until it was too late? What was she really like? Now removed from her presence, he can with some detachment seek to understand both their marriage and the person that is himself. He does not perform this work of understanding another's reality particularly well, but he does carry out the moral task of piercing the dense fog of his relationships by means of an interior conversation.

In each of her novels Murdoch invites her readers to become engaged in a similar dialogue by reflecting on their characters and situations. In her novel *The Unicorn*, several fictional characters come to different conclusions about the female protagonist, and readers are challenged to draw their own. These assessments are to be moral ones—efforts to penetrate the fantasy created by each person's own self-concern. Indirectly, this helps the readers improve in their ability to penetrate their own fantasy-world by training them to pay attention to the particular realities—persons and social situations—they encounter in their daily round of earning a living, being alone or part of a household, being a citizen, growing old and facing mortality.

The task of paying attention is demanding. It can be performed only as one gains some freedom from self-importance and self-concern ("turned in on oneself," as Luther put it) and from our many, often competing desires that prevent us from attending to others. What takes place in the world about us matters. Its reality begins to emerge as we begin to experience ourselves as one reality among many. Then the world's goodness, its fascinating splendor, begins to reveal itself as the object of a perfect love—God's.

Only through the experience of goodness can reality pierce our fantasy world. Once we see that there is a healing reality independent of us, and from whose goodness we are cut off by our own egocentrism, then our conscience is restored. Because of our egocentricity we need to meditate in order to move ourselves off-center, and we need a great deal of practice at paying attention. Every moment, thought, and action either contributes to or detracts from our ability to pay attention to what is before us.

Simone Weil, who deeply influenced Iris Murdoch, stressed the value of school studies for developing this power of attention:

> Attention consists of suspending our thought, leaving it detached, empty, and ready to be penetrated by the object [of study]....Above all our thought should be empty, waiting, not seeking anything, but ready to receive in its naked truth the object that is to penetrate it.[2]

To empty ourselves in order to be "penetrated" by the object of our study means that in the first place we must want to know the truth or to know the correct answer. This desire is frequently not our motivation in study; instead, we want to receive a good grade, to pass an examination, to win success at school, to improve our chances for a good job, and so on. We also approach various subjects with different attitudes—some we like, other we don't. But to receive the truth we must have an attitude of desiring to know the truth about everything we study regardless of our tastes. We must suspend our wishes, our desires, and even our previous views to accept the results of our study, whatever they may be, especially when its results run counter to what we expect.

In the second place, Weil writes, we must examine carefully the school tasks in which we have failed or done poorly without seeking excuses for our mistakes, taking seriously our teacher's corrections and trying to understand the source of our mistakes. We are greatly tempted not to examine carefully the inadequacy or mediocrity of our work because we do not like to be in the wrong or to linger on our faults. Yet this care is necessary if we wish to improve, and it is indispensable to learning what is true of whatever we are studying. Think how a skater or a baseball player repeats a movement again and again in order to perfect it—only so can they learn to perform well. Care in overcoming faults is just as indispensable in learning how to pay attention, to understand correctly, and to know the truth about anything. Careful examination of any failure or inadequate performance also teaches humility. The "fat, relentless ego," as Iris Murdoch calls it, is brought under control by this evidence that we are not making genuine contact with what we want to study and it helps get us out of the way of what is there to be known.

To learn how to pay attention it is not essential that one get top grades. Anyone who genuinely and persistently tries to understand and grasp what is true, regardless of his or her ability or success, can profit. The genuine desire to understand and know helps one to become a person who can be attentive to whatever is present—attentive not only to academic study, but also to people, situations, and one's own actions and motives. The persistent effort we put into trying to learn, including learning from our mistakes, rewards us with increased power to pay attention to anything, including the holy things of prayer, meditation, and contemplation.

Attention is not muscular effort— such as contracting your brow, holding your breath, or stiffening your muscles. It is a matter of interest, desire, wanting to know. This usually develops as we start to find learning pleasurable. Similarly, as we read, pray, and listen to scripture attentively, we increase in our desire to change the kind of person we are, we come to regret our failures, we wish to become more loving toward others, and we begin to long for God.

The beginnings are small, just like seeds that are sown. But as Jesus said, "The kingdom of heaven is like a mustard seed that someone took and sowed in his field; it is the smallest of all the seeds, but when it has grown it is the greatest of shrubs and becomes a tree, so that birds of the air come and make nests in its branches" (Matt. 13:31-32). If we have only the smallest desire for God, but develop the power to pay attention, we will find that Jesus' remark about the mustard seed will begin to come true in our own lives.

∴ ∴

Traditionally, attentiveness in contemplation and meditation has been one of the ways that Christians increase their knowledge of God. Around the time of Descartes in the seventeenth century, however, meditative and contemplative attention (a path to knowledge in the philosophy of Plato and Aristotle) gradually disappeared. Instead, knowledge became an instrument for controlling nature in order to produce the effects we want. Francis Bacon, in his *Novum Organum* ("new instrument," in contrast to the "old instrument" for knowledge), derided the Aristotelianism of the universities. He claimed that Aristotle's understanding of causality gave us no insight into "the springs of nature"—that is, into causes we could use to produce changes in nature and bend it to our purposes. Bacon sought knowledge that would give us power over nature. After the time of Bacon, ever-increasing theoretical and technological knowledge meant we could continually transform our methods of production and transportation, yielding the levels of industry and commerce that we now take for granted. The achievement is breathtaking, but we are increasingly aware of an imbalance: nature is susceptible to considerable manipulation and control, but there are limits to what can be achieved in this way.

Nor is God subject to our control. The only way we may know God is by responding to what God does as creator and to God's loving intentions for our lives. Simone Weil showed us how the Christian doctrines of trinity, incarnation, and atonement, which are beyond the grasp of the intellect, can nonetheless be loved. When these doctrines are loved, they illumine the mind so that it can gain an understanding of our world and our life in the world in relation to God. Although God is beyond the *direct* grasp of the intellect, through loving attention to God's creation and to the revelation of scripture we can increase in our understanding of God indirectly. Both nature and scripture mediate God's presence.

In meditation and contemplation Christians seek to grow in knowledge and love of God by increasing their understanding of what it is they believe and love. As Anselm stated in his treatise *Cur Deus Homo,* a work in which he sought to understand why it was fitting that God should become a human being, Christians "do not expect to come to faith through reason, but they hope to be gladdened by the understanding and contemplation of the things they believe."[3] Anselm knew we cannot comprehend God's nature, nor the central doctrines of God as trinity, creator, and Word incarnate. Our understanding of these mysteries is limited. But divine truths can be thought about, and some understanding achieved, when they are attended to lovingly.

In seeking to know God, writes Maximus the Confessor, pay attention to the things about God, "his eternity, immensity, infinity, his goodness, wisdom and power which creates, governs, and judges creatures. For that person is a great theologian who searches out the principles of these things, however much or little."[4] As we seek to understand and contemplate all things in relation to God, the mind is brought to the ultimate reality of God, who surpasses all understanding. Our loving, prayerful reflection increases our love for God. We ascend and come closer to God; God descends and comes closer to us.

The contemplative life is possible only when the heart and mind are changed through repentance and an increasing love for God, as we become more integrated and focused in our desires. In short, some maturity in the active life is necessary. Then in our meditation and contemplation we are increasingly drawn into participation in the divine life. Part of our repentance is intellectual—a recognition that God is above the capacity of our minds. To be known, God must come to us. So it is no use trying to set up experiments to detect God and learn something about God that way. Only an openness to God, a loving attention to God's creation and the particular revelation of God's intentions in scripture, most fully present in Jesus Christ, gives the mind a degree of understanding of God. Through that understanding we increase in our love.

Anyone who has begun to learn to pay attention and to long for God's presence is capable of contemplation in a sustained and persistent way. According to the traditional threefold way, the objects of our loving contemplation should be the two books of God, nature and scripture. Through them God communicates with us. The word of God spoken at creation structures and sustains the universe. Creation itself reflects God's power, wisdom, and goodness, as Maximus the Confessor states:

> We do not know God from his being but from his magnificent works and his Providence for beings. Through these as through mirrors we perceive his infinite goodness and wisdom and power.[5]

We can detect vestiges or traces of the word of God that formed and sustains the universe. By prayerful reflection on them, that Word becomes active in us, forming and reforming us into the divine likeness by increasing our knowledge of the power, wisdom, and goodness of God. Not only do we come to perceive the universe as a great gift, a sign of God's generosity, but we also receive it as a gift by becoming more generous ourselves.

Human beings not only reflect God's power, wisdom, and goodness, as does all creation, they are created in God's image. However, we have so damaged the image that we are unable to restore it or even understand what it is. Jesus Christ actualized this image in his person and life; he not only reveals it, but enables it to be restored in us. He unites himself to us, and by that union our lives increasingly become shaped into his likeness. By reflecting on our life as it is being reformed by him, we meet the Word of God within ourselves.

Growing in knowledge and love of God through the book of nature is made possible for us through the incarnation. The Word of God incarnate is present and active in us, reforming our broken nature whether we realize it or not. Knowledge of the Word of God incarnate is gained only through the book of scripture, and through worship, preaching, and teaching based on scripture. The scriptures give us an understanding of God's intentions and providence that we could not receive from the book of nature. As such it is an indispensable guide for accurate reflection on nature, which is both the external world and our own human nature. But throughout our meditation on the two books of God, it is the same Word of God who communicates with us and who works within us, refashioning us so that we may increasingly know and love God and our neighbor.

The work of the Holy Spirit in purifying our passions, guiding us, and filling us with charity and yearning for God is beautifully captured in the late medieval hymn *Discendi, Amor santo* by Bianco da Siena:

Come down, O Love divine, seek thou this soul of mine,
And visit it with thine own ardour glowing;
O Comforter, draw near, within my heart appear,
And kindle it, thy holy flame bestowing.

O let it freely burn, till earthly passions turn
To dust and ashes in its heat consuming.
And let thy glorious light shine ever on my sight,
And clothe me round, the while my path illuming.

Let holy charity mine outward vesture be,
And lowliness become mine inner clothing;
True lowliness of heart, which takes the humbler part,
And o'er its own shortcomings weeps with loathing.

And so the yearning strong, with which the soul will long,
Shall far outpass the power of human telling;
For none can guess its grace,
Till he become a place wherein the Holy Spirit makes his
dwelling.[6]

In the following chapters we will examine precisely what we are to put before our minds in meditation and contemplation from the two books of God.

Notes

1. Maximus the Confessor, *Four Hundred Chapters on Love*, George C. Berthold, trans. (Mahwah, N. J.: Paulist Press, 1985), 1.77; see also 2.26.
2. Simone Weil, *Waiting for God* (New York: Harper & Row, 1973), 111-112.
3. Quoted in E. R. Fairweather, ed., *A Scholastic Miscellany* (New York: Macmillan, 1970), 101.
4. Maximus, *Four Hundred Chapters*, 2.27.
5. *Ibid.*, 1.96.
6. Hymn 115 in *The Church Hymnary*, 3rd edition, Richard Frederick Littledale, trans. (Oxford: Oxford University Press, 1973).

CHAPTER EIGHT

THE BOOK
OF NATURE

For centuries Basil of Caesarea's nine sermons on the opening chapters of Genesis—the *Hexaemeron*, or *Six Days*—were the most celebrated of his works. Today, however, Basil and the other theologians who emphasized contemplation of nature as a way to increase our knowledge and love of God are brushed aside, even by Christian scholars. Basil is dismissed because in his exposition of Genesis he employs the scientific thinking of his day—although on those grounds we should also dismiss Genesis itself, since it too reflects an understanding of the world that is scientifically out-of-date.

Nonetheless, we must take this dismissive attitude seriously because it is so widespread today. For many theologians, the study of nature is no longer a way to know and love God; the notion that God is directly responsible for the operations of nature seems outdated to them. Consequently, they have also rejected natural theology, which seeks to prove God's existence and goodness from the natural world.

In *Christian Belief in a Postmodern World* I described recent developments in science, especially in cosmology, that have made us aware of the limits of science. According to the Big Bang theory, our universe began some fifteen or so billion years ago, expanding from a very small, dense mass. This has prompted many people to realize the soundness of what seem like a child's questions, "Why do we have a universe at all? Why is the universe the way it is, rather than something else?" These questions cannot be answered by science. Science gains its knowledge from studying the universe that already exists, so it cannot tell us why the universe has these laws or why we have a universe at all. Science simply takes the universe as given, and describes the processes that work in it; it does not exclude the possibility of a creator who ordered the universe in the first place.

Basil's contemplation of nature for spiritual purposes does not rest on the specific scientific details of his day. In their essentials, Basil's teachings on Genesis are as valid and insightful for spiritual growth in our day as they were in his. As we will see, Basil and theologians like him—Bonaventure, Julian of Norwich, Hugh of St. Victor, Simone Weil—rely on the Bible to guide them in their understanding of nature. Without faith in Christ and a love for God, we cannot read nature as God's book.

As far as natural theology goes, philosophers and theologians since Kant have all too often assumed that because we cannot conclusively prove God's existence from nature, the natural world itself cannot increase our understanding and love for God. But proof of God's existence from nature (natural theology) and the contemplation of nature are not the same thing.

The only barrier to the contemplation of nature for spiritual purposes lies is our motives. Jesus said, "Where your treasure is, there your heart will be also" (Luke 12:34). Our treasure is whatever we think of as our good. If God has become what we treasure and so desire, then we can begin to find in our meditation on the natural world those things that increase our understanding and love for God.

Purity of heart—the desire for God for God's own sake—is necessary in every age in order to learn to read nature as God's book. This should make it clear that the book of nature is never read in isolation from the book of scripture; scriptural teaching leads to faith, and it is from scripture that we learn of Christ's commandments. Through obedience, our desires are so shaped that God becomes our treasure, and only then do we receive the universe as a great gift.

In early Christian literature God's rule was referred to as God's *oikonomia*, or "economy," the term for household management. We live in God's household, under God's care, learning much about God through a careful and grateful examination of his gift. For the ancient church, the universe was perceived as a great gift, a revelation of the invisible God and the result of God's power, wisdom, and goodness. We can better understand and admire God's power, wisdom, and goodness as we increase in our knowledge of the world's order, harmony, and beauty— God's glory. In the Greek of the New Testament, unlike classical Greek, the word "glory" is used to mean "presence." God is present in and through creatures, but is not contained in them. All creatures reveal God's continual creative and providential activity.

Not only was this teaching widespread in the early and medieval church, it can also be found in Protestant reformers like John Calvin. In Book I of his *Institutes of the Christian Religion*, Calvin claims that simply by looking at the world it should be evident to us that God is its source. Since we are blinded by sin, however, the light of God is scattered and fragmented into many rays, as though we suffered from astigmatism, and we cannot see clearly. But when through God's grace we come to faith, we are able to see the world as God's good creation. By "faith" Calvin means a mature faith, one no longer distorted by our passions. Only then do we actually perceive nature as God's gift and glory.

✌ ↝

Theologians like Basil of Caesarea and Bonaventure used the contemplation of nature, including both the natural world and human nature, as a way to increase their love and knowledge of God. In the nine sermons he preached on the opening chapter of Genesis, Basil offers his theological reflections on the creation of the world as the subject matter of meditation for ordinary

Christians. He appeals to Moses as his authority—Moses, held to be the author of Genesis, spent forty years of his life as a shepherd and was well-acquainted with the natural world. When he was called by God to lead the children of Israel out of Egypt, God appeared to him in a burning bush; later, Moses met God in a dark cloud. These encounters gave Moses the authority to impart to us in Genesis what he had learned from God, namely, that the whole world has its origin in God.

The single opening verse of Genesis, "In the beginning when God created the heavens and the earth," is the basis for Basil's first sermon. From this verse, Basil tells us, we learn that "an intelligent cause presided at the birth of the universe" rather than, as the Greek philosophers taught, randomness or chance. Furthermore, the world was created in order to show only "a very small part of the power of the Creator. In the same way that the potter, after having made with equal pains a great number of vessels, has not exhausted either his art or his talent."[1] If the world does have a beginning, Basil continues, who is responsible for this beginning? That is exactly where we are today in our philosophy and science. After several centuries of claiming that science held the key to everything, and the universe has always been here, today we know from science itself that the universe had a definite beginning. Thus everyone is faced with the question Basil raised: "If the world had a beginning, then who gave it that beginning?"

Because of this revelation, Basil tells us, we are no longer doomed to study nature without ever finding its source. All is not given over to chance or to necessity. Instead, for everyone who receives the truth that in the beginning God created the heavens and earth, the world is a school in which to learn about God. All creation is "the school where reasonable souls exercise themselves, the training ground where they learn to know God; since by the sight of visible and sensible things the mind is led, as by a hand, to the contemplation of invisible things."[2]

For Basil the universe is a work of art for all to behold, like a splendid sculpture or a harmonious symphony. Furthermore, we can know and use nature's order for our reflections on God without scientific knowledge. The mechanisms and laws by which the universe operates are all the creation of God and completely dependent on God, whether we understand them or not. Even without understanding the mechanisms of nature, the visible world is such a glorious work of art that its marvelous order is enough for us to praise God.

The only shortcoming I see in Basil's sermons on nature is his criticism of those whose curiosity leads them to investigate nature's workings. He claims we can know God's goodness, wisdom, and power without such knowledge. This theological disincentive for the scientific study of nature, however, is balanced by his other emphasis: when we do gain some knowledge of an inner working of nature, we marvel all the more over God's creation. In offering the natural world as the subject matter of meditation, Basil tells his hearers what they are to look for as they go about their daily work. In his fourth sermon he exclaims:

> I want creation to fill you with so much admiration that everywhere, wherever you may be, the least plant may bring to you the clear remembrance of the Creator. If you see grass, think of human nature, and remember the comparison of the wise Isaiah, "All flesh is grass, and all the goodliness thereof is as the flower of the field."[3]

Basil devotes at least two sermons to this kind of reflection, which could be dismissed as moralizing but to me makes good sense. We tend to forget that we are mortal creatures and we need to be reminded of our destiny in the great, unbounded Lord of creation. Furthermore, Basil always relies on scripture to guide him in his reading of nature, frequently praising Jesus Christ as the Wisdom of God that is reflected in the structure of the creation. In the long preamble to the sixth sermon Basil makes it clear that in order to receive knowledge of God from nature, we must be on a spiritual journey and not mere spectators.

Nine centuries later the Franciscan friar Bonaventure treated both the world of nature and human nature in his thirteenth-century treatise, *The Soul's Journey into God*. As in Basil's writing about creation, the figure of Christ is central; with Bonaventure, the route of contemplation into the life of God is opened to us by a burning love for the crucified Christ. The heart-felt meditation in the book's prologue is a characteristic example of the Franciscan emphasis on Christ's suffering love. We ascend to God by means of six "rungs" of a ladder, corresponding to the six wings of the seraph in St. Francis's vision. Two wings symbolize the vestiges of God in the physical universe, two wings the image of God in humanity, and two stand for the names of God as Being and Good. The seventh and last stage of contemplation is the crucified Christ; through Christ's crucifixion, we may finally enter and be united to the life of God, Father, Son, and Holy Spirit. Yet this journey is impossible for us unless we long for God and make Christ the focus of our lives. Without Christ's redeeming work, there is no possibility of ascent to God.

Bonaventure has much to say about our growth in knowledge and love of God through the contemplation of nature. In his first chapter of *The Soul's Journey into God* Bonaventure lists the seven properties of creatures on which we are to meditate: their origin, magnitude, multitude, beauty, fullness, activity, and order. Meditation on each one of these increases our awareness of God's power, wisdom, and goodness. Let us consider one of them, the magnitude of the universe, and adapt Bonaventure's meditation to our present-day knowledge.

The people of ancient Israel did not realize how immense the universe was, but they were so impressed by its greatness that it amazed them God should take human beings so seriously:

When I look at your heavens, the work of your fingers,
    the moon and stars that you have established;
what are human beings that you are mindful of them,
    mortals that you care for them? (Ps. 8:3-4)

Only in this century has it been established that stars are grouped into galaxies—large islands of stars. In our galaxy the star nearest to our sun is 4.3 light years away. It takes light one hundred thousand years to cross our galaxy, and even these figures are dwarfed by the fact that there are a billion or more galaxies. As one scientist writes, "Galaxies are to astronomers what atoms are to physicists."[4] What is more, stars are still being formed and the universe is still expanding. The light we see through telescopes from galaxies not visible to the naked eye show us what the universe was like in the distant past; in galactic astronomy, we are constantly looking into the past, not the present.

The enormous size of the universe, the immense variety of life forms and species throughout creation, the surpassing beauty of the world—no matter how far our telescopes allow us to see or how great the magnification of our microscopes, whatever we see is beautiful. All this beauty seems to have no role in our evolution—it is gratuitous, or better yet, a gift. The English mystic Julian of Norwich had a vision of creation as God must see it, no larger than a hazelnut in the palm of her hand:

> I was amazed that it could last, for I thought it was so little that it could suddenly fall into nothing. And I was answered in my understanding: It lasts and always will, because God loves it; and thus everything has being through the love of God.[5]

As a source of contemplation, the natural world especially recommended itself to Bonaventure because of St. Francis's love of creation. "The Canticle of Brother Sun" is his hymn of praise that calls on sun, moon, stars, wind, and water—all parts of God's creation—to praise the Lord God. At the end of the hymn he comes to death: "Praised be you, Lord God, for our Sister Bodily Death, from whom no living man can escape." Death reminds us that we are creatures; the sun, moon, stars and all the rest are our brothers and sisters. We praise God for death because it helps us to recognize that we are not only creatures, but God's creatures. We are able to rejoice that God has opened our eyes to respond to his power, wisdom, and goodness throughout creation. A vast and deep chasm separates the insight that we must die and the recognition that we are creatures of God—it is the difference between stoical acceptance of a hard fact and rejoicing in all that exists.

At Trinity Church in Princeton is a small stained glass window made up of small panels, each devoted to the sun, moon, wind, water, fire, and earth. At the very top, visible only when you stand well back, is a small panel depicting Sister Bodily Death, who peers down on the others. It is well she is more difficult to see; our lives should not be dominated by the thought of death. But an awareness of our mortality is necessary for us to develop a mature faith in God, one than can withstand injury, accident, disease, aging, and death; otherwise, we live in an illusory world. Christ, who called himself the truth, dwells only in truth, not in illusion. His way leads us to life as we face hard truths while trusting in him.

⌣ ⌣

In meditating on God's power, wisdom, and goodness as revealed in nature, we are meditating on what is *outside* of us. Another source of meditation is to look inward toward our own human nature. Since humanity is created in the image of God, the "inward way" gives us a more intimate knowledge of God. I will not explore Bonaventure's reflections on the inward way because I am not sure that the philosophical assumptions behind them make them useful for today. Instead, I will give some reflections of my own. All accounts of the inward way rely on the fact that we are made in the divine image, and that Christ, by uniting himself with us, is restoring that image.

One place we meet and know God within ourselves is through our sheer existence. We can also realize that we are creatures of God by meditating on the two thieves who were crucified alongside Jesus. They remind us that in one sense we are no different. We deceive ourselves into thinking we belong to ourselves, but of course we don't—we belong to God, on whom we depend for every instant of our lives. The only difference between the two thieves who were crucified with Jesus is that one of them repented and the other did not.

Which kind of thief are we? If we are a repentant one, we must constantly be reminded that we belong to God by our obedience. As Maximus the Confessor pointed out, we are sometimes careless in our obedience and so do not show forth Christ's presence in our lives. We must not only obey the commandments, but also have a sense of belonging to God in our most fundamental attitude toward ourselves. The more we are conscious that we belong to God, the more we meet God in our sheer existence. God is present to us in every breath and thought.

We can have the same experience in those moments when we allow all that is extraneous and accidental to drop away, leaving us with our essential identity. For example, I once glanced out of a window and saw a colleague passing by, someone I had always found colorless, dull, and boring. I thought to myself, "I am so glad that I am not like him. How glad I am that I am lively, charming, and interesting!" Then it struck me. "You and he are essentially alike. All the things that you think distinguish you from him are not *essential*. Essentially, you are both creatures." When the thought "You and he are essentially alike" entered my heart, I found myself released from my disdain; I felt a deep bond with that man. In that awareness of our common existence, I came in that moment nearer to God, and nearer to resembling God's love for his creatures.

In my own way I lived the story Jesus once told about a Pharisee who in the Temple prayed, "God, I thank you that I am not like other people: thieves, rogues, adulterers, or even like this tax collector. I fast twice a week; I give a tenth of all my income" (Luke 18:10-13). Happily, I also experienced the removal of evil. I never thought of this man in the same way ever again, and at times I use this experience as a reminder.

When we meet God in these ways, and find our evil evaporating, we also recognize that we ourselves are irreplaceable. We can see this in the remarkable story of Adam and Eve. After they disobeyed, God did not destroy them and make new creatures, as he could have done; instead, he continued to try to fulfill his purpose through them. We find it very hard to believe that we are irreplaceable. We have so damaged the image and likeness of God that we do not recognize it in ourselves or in others. We live in the accidental that divides us, rather than in the essential that unites us and leads us to God's presence.

Simone Weil brings together the inward and the outward way in a manner that is unique. For her the universe consists of several levels: on the bottom there is merely space and on the next there is matter, which is extremely small in comparison. It takes light traveling 186,000 miles per second two million years to reach us from the nearest galaxy. The next level of the universe is living matter, which is only a small fraction of all matter. For example, on our planet life is found only on its surface area and in the sea; the rest is lifeless. Among living things, human beings have the highest level of intelligence, but the vast majority of our thoughts are self-centered. We tend to see, feel, and understand everything from our point of view. From time to time we escape from our egocentricity and perceive things as they really are, free of the distorting effect of our wishes, interests, fears, and self-importance, and we learn from that experience how small we are compared to the vastness of the universe, and the vastness of its indifference toward us.

This happens because we receive divine grace, which lets us recognize that those occasional moments of escape from egocentric thoughts and feelings are the key to the meaning of the whole universe. We realize that there is a reality which is good, and which seeks to enter the universe in our own person. However much we may learn from physics, chemistry, biology, sociology, and psychology, it is at the core of ourselves that we find the meaning and significance of the whole. Without that, no other studies can yield meaning and significance.

৴: ৴

A lesser-known strain in the Christian tradition also saw reflection on technology, work, and human skill as part of the contemplation of the natural world, and it is to this tradition I want to turn now. The contemplative study of the book of nature I have just outlined is better known in Christian spirituality than the more "active" approach represented by technology and

THE BOOK OF NATURE ~ 119

commerce—the use of nature for human purposes—which shapes our lives so powerfully today.

In 1120 one of the great contemplatives, Hugh of St. Victor, composed a major book called the *Didascalicon*, or *Instruction*, which took a highly positive view of labor and technology. He argued that the technological improvement of life on earth is part of our restoration from the Fall. Although the fall destroyed our ability to know and obey God, through the work of Christ that capacity is being restored. Technology and commerce help restore us to our proper relationship to nature, which is one of stewardship, and which improves our earthly life so we may approximate more fully our original condition in paradise.

Although Hugh made a distinctive and influential contribution, he is only part of a long tradition in Christianity that looked to the renewal of human beings made possible by Christ.[6] Union with Christ is so fundamental a form of renewal that in the New Testament it is called *a new creation* (Eph. 4:24; Col. 3:10; 2 Cor. 5:17). Christians are to be engaged in overcoming the effects of the Fall that obliterated the image of God and to strive to realize more and more the divine likeness. In St. Basil's *Hexaemeron*, moreover, the theologian connects the work of his hearers, many of whom were craftspeople, with the productive work of God. The "productive" arts, such as architecture, especially mirror God's creativity because they endure and continue to show the "industrious intelligence" of the architect or builder. Basil honors human work as an image of the divine work. Since the productive work of men and women is linked to the restoration of the divine image in us and growth into the divine likeness, productive work is directly related to our sanctification.

The medieval emphasis on physical labor, which was so much a part of the restoration of the image of God in the monastic rule of life, was closely connected to the improvement of farming and other technological innovations. Hugh of St. Victor saw technology as part of the human quest for knowledge. There are three types of knowledge: theoretical (mathematics, physics, and theology); practical (politics, ethics, and economics); and technological or mechanical (fabric-making, armament, commerce, agriculture, hunting, medicine, and theatrics). To make technology a category of knowledge is already to have elevated its status, since for Hugh (as for Augustine, who greatly influenced him) all knowledge ultimately leads to God. This is extremely daring, since it means that technology has the potential to be spiritual. Hugh makes this connection explicit when he points out that the different types of knowledge all serve to mitigate the results of the Fall: theoretical knowledge as a remedy for ignorance, practical knowledge for vice, technological knowledge for physical weakness. Technology is part of the spiritual task of restoring our condition before the fall.

Because we are earthly beings with a supernatural destiny, our knowledge must also include the technology that enables us to safeguard and make more pleasant our earthly existence. Therefore for Hugh the spiritual is not defined in *opposition* to the physical, as it is with some spiritual theologians, for to treat technology as a type of knowledge is largely to overcome the ancient contrast between mind and matter. In this respect he is closer to Basil than to Bonaventure, who neglected this aspect of the book of nature.

Hugh has a major place in most contemporary studies of medieval ideas about technology, but he was not an isolated figure. Influenced by Augustine, he drew on a long tradition and had considerable influence in his turn.[7] His work continued at the monastery of St. Victor under the leadership of Richard and Godfrey, and many direct references to his ideas can be found in figures such as Roger Bacon, the thirteenth-century Franciscan scientist. Godfrey made an important addition to Hugh's thought by connecting the mechanical arts to the ascetical discipline of the ancient monastic tradition. The mechanical arts, he argued, require a training and discipline that helps to direct and control our diverse and scattered passions. Somewhat as Simone Weil argued that school studies help us develop the faculty of attention, Godfrey held that training in the mechanical arts helps train us to be obedient to God's commandments. If properly exercised, commercial life could help in the development of virtue: merchants could think of themselves as monks in the world.[8]

Martin Luther insisted that all vocations which serve the good of one's neighbor are divine vocations. Each Christian practicing a vocation, whether within or without the household, is being a priest in mediating Christ to others. This move from the spiritual value of crafts to Luther's view of vocation was revolutionary: it transformed people's relationship toward the church. However, the understanding of the spiritual life as vitally connected to the mechanical arts is a natural evolution of Hugh's ideas, just as Hugh's ideas are a natural development of ideas reaching back to the theologians of the early church.

In the twentieth century, Simone Weil put skilled work at the center of the spiritual life when she wrote, "Our age has its own particular mission, or vocation—the creation of a civilization founded upon the spiritual nature of work."[9] For Weil, work was crucial to human redemption. Her thought developed in stages, beginning with her doctoral thesis *Science and Perception in Descartes,* where she suggested that an alternative concept of knowledge was needed. Modern science had moved exclusively in a direction requiring lengthy intellectual study, while the mass of working people had effectively been cut off from knowledge of the natural world because they lacked means and often the aptitude for abstract study. This made workers dependent on an intellectual elite, who increasingly designed factories in such a way as to reduce the skill workers needed to produce goods.

In her highly sophisticated analysis, Weil argued that since there is no separation between thought and sensations, proper attention to our sensations give us knowledge of the workings of nature. Craftspeople such as weavers, embroiderers, and lacemakers use their bodies in such a way that an orderly series of sensations are produced. Their very tools become the projection of their bodies as they learn to manipulate both bodies and tools to produce the desired results. Skill is achieved with training and practice; by means of an apprenticeship skilled workers not only learn a trade, but gain a practical knowledge of the natural world. Knowledge of nature through skilled work is an alternative route for a knowledge of nature that can be followed by the mass of people, in contrast to an abstract route available only to a relative few.

Although there would always be need of managers, increasing the need for skilled workers would allow large numbers of people to have scope in their working lives for some self-direction. What makes factory work inhuman and brutal is large-scale production with machinery that requires little skill or intelligence to run. When work is simply the application of brute force by unskilled workers, the workers themselves are brutalized by labor that gives no satisfaction, no dignity, and no practical knowledge of the principles of nature. Work becomes solely a way to make money, deadening the rest of life.

Those who are fortunate enough to be engaged in skilled work gain a practical knowledge of the natural world as a functioning, interacting whole. This gives them one of the crucial ingredients for the spiritual life: they can be taught to make contact with God in and through their work. Through pleasant and unpleasant sensations, caused by interactions with nature, they have contact with God, the source of nature. In a possible allusion to George Herbert's poem "The Elixir," Weil says that nature takes on the transparency of a window pane. Rather than looking *at* nature, we see *through* it, and "as soon as we feel this obedience with our whole being, we see God."[10]

For Weil, obtaining knowledge of God through a practical understanding of the operations of the natural world is not limited to artisans or skilled workers, although they are particularly well-placed. All of us have access to this understanding because all of us experience the workings of nature on our bodies. It requires us to learn, however, that God is as much present to us in the pain inflicted by nature as in the pleasure it causes, as Weil wrote,

Through joy the beauty of the world penetrates our soul. Through suffering it penetrates our body. We could no more become friends of God through joy alone than one becomes a ship's captain by studying books on navigation. The body plays a part in all apprenticeships.[11]

It is clear that, for Weil, to study nature in order to increase our knowledge of God is not merely to interpret, understand, or try to prove the existence of God. It is to *do* something—to yield ourselves to God through our love of this world, a world that is difficult to love, however beautiful it may be, when it injures us. This too is an imitation of God's love, when through his incarnation he yielded his very flesh on the cross.

After centuries of neglect, the book of nature is now available for our spiritual growth in the knowledge and love of God. Not only may we draw upon the spiritual writings of the past, but we may also integrate them with modern knowledge. Modern science in particular, far from being a barrier, can actually enhance our awareness of God's power, wisdom, and goodness.

Notes

1. Basil of Caesarea, *Hexaemeron* in *Nicene and Post-Nicene Fathers*, 2nd series, Blomfield Jackson, ed. and trans. (Grand Rapids: Eerdmans, 1983), 8:52.

2. *Ibid.*, 55.

3. *Ibid.*, 76.

4. Alan Sandage, *National Geographic Atlas* (1983), 6.

5. Julian of Norwich, *Showings*, Edmund Colledge and James Walsh, trans. (New York: Paulist Press, 1978), 130-131.

6. See *Bonaventure: The Soul's Journey into God, The Tree of Life, The Life of St. Francis*, Ewert Cousins, trans. (New York: Paulist Press, 1978), 28.

7. In *The Idea of Reform* (New York: Harper & Row, 1967), Gerhart Ladner traces the idea of reform and renewal in western civilization to the fundamentally Christian conviction of human renovation that is made possible by Christ.

8. Richard H. Tawney, in *Religion and the Spirit of Capitalism* (New York: Harcourt, Brace & Co., 1926), argued that those engaged in commerce in the Netherlands and England in the late seventeenth century believed that the very practice of commerce helped develop virtue.

9. Simone Weil, *The Need for Roots*, Arthur Wills, trans. (New York: Harper & Row, 1971), 96.

10. Simone Weil, *Science, Necessity and the Love of God*, Richard Rees, trans. (London: Oxford University Press, 1968), 180.

11. Simone Weil, *Waiting for God* (New York: Harper & Row, 1973), 180.

CHAPTER NINE

THE BOOK OF SCRIPTURE

In this chapter we are going to examine the role of scripture in the spiritual journey, just as in the previous chapter we examined the role of nature in knowing and loving God. Our focus is the primary ancient and medieval method of scriptural interpretation to understand the role of the Bible in the journey to God. Although the use of scripture for meditation involves using the mind, its main purpose is to shape the soul, the entire person. Through the prayerful reading of scripture we seek to gain knowledge of God; in the contemplative tradition, this ardent longing and search can ultimately lead to a direct experience of God, either in the form of momentary ecstasy or a sense of God's habitual presence. This reading of scripture, however, is only possible for those who are engaged in the fight against evil in their hearts and earnestly desire to follow Christ.

Through the meditative reading of the Bible we apply the scriptures to our own moral lives, and eventually this reading shapes us in such a way that we can receive greater knowledge of God through the scriptures. As we allow the knowledge of God gained through the scriptures to guide us, nourishing the heart and mind, we are increasingly formed into the likeness of God. Spiritual growth brings illumination of new and deeper meanings hidden in the Bible.

In reading scripture on our spiritual journey we are to read with the intention of hearing. Etymologically the word "obedience" means "to act out of hearing"; it is to do what you hear said to you. A good working knowledge of the words of scripture, and the understanding gained through sermons, teaching, and worship can help us to read so that we can act on what we hear. Since our spiritual growth is a journey and since we are in different places as we journey, as we read the scriptures we are to listen to what is intended for us at that moment in time. Depending on the place we have reached, what the scriptures say to us is often new.

In his famous Rule, Benedict often prefaces his instructions with the remark "Listen, my son." Learning to listen is vital because to be spiritual is to be in an obedient relationship, to be responsive. The beginning of spirituality—the beginning of being responsive—is learning to listen. It is the beginning of a relationship to God which the twelfth-century abbess Hildegard of Bingen described as, "I dance with you as my lead." Reading scriptures of itself will not change us, but responding to the scriptures will. Reading the scriptures gives us the chance to respond, to dance with God as our lead.

The primary method of interpreting scripture in the ancient and medieval church was based on what is called "the fourfold meaning of scripture": the literal (or historical), the allegorical (or typological), the moral (or tropological), and the mystical (or anagogical). In his *Conferences* John Cassian reports at length the teachings of Abba Nesteros, a desert father of the early fourth century, about whom little is known save that he is referred to as a friend of the famous St. Anthony. His teaching on how we receive spiritual knowledge, however, is a very valuable example of the role of the Bible in the spiritual life because Nesteros presents it within the context of the threefold way, which finds its culmination in the presence of God. But even more important for our purposes are the examples he gives of the fourfold interpretation of scripture.[1]

Today our understanding of this ancient mode of reading scripture is often distorted because we mistakenly assume it is limited to allegory, such as the patristic interpretation of the scarlet cord in Joshua 2:18 as the blood of Christ. This lack of understanding, along with a neglect of the larger context of the role of scripture in the search for knowledge of God, discourages the use of this discipline. Yet this fourfold method is modeled on the practice of Paul and other writers of the New Testament and, according to the gospels, on that of Jesus himself.

Knowledge of the Bible is of two kinds, which Nesteros distinguishes as practical and theoretical knowledge. Practical knowledge is connected to the moral life and its improvement, while theoretical knowledge comes from contemplation. In turn, this theoretical knowledge of the Bible is of two kinds, the historical (or "literal"), and the spiritual. Two examples Nesteros gives of the historical sense are drawn from the writings of Paul:

> For I handed on to you as of first importance what I in turn had received: that Christ died for our sins in accordance with the scriptures, and that he was buried, and that he was raised on the third day in accordance with the scriptures, and that he appeared to Cephas, then to the twelve. (I Cor. 15:3-5)

> God sent his Son, born of a woman, born under the law, in order to redeem those who were under the law. (Gal. 4:4-5)

This historical sense is part of the broader category of the "literal" (from *littera*, the Latin word for *letter*) sense of scripture: what the text literally *says*, or as Nesteros put it, "what is declared by the very words." This is not what we mean by "literal," since for us the literal does not include the metaphorical. But when Christians of the ancient and medieval church came upon a metaphorical saying like "I am the door of the sheep," they understood the text in its most literal sense, metaphor and all.

Another difference between Nesteros's understanding of scripture and ours is that, for us, the text—"what is declared by the very words"—of scripture can be understood without actually believing what it says. Anyone can understand, for example, that it is a good thing to follow Jesus' example and teaching, renouncing passions such as gluttony, anger, and avarice, and loving our neighbors as ourselves; these are the parts of the threefold way. Merely to understand these words does not require action or even belief on our part. Yet this is not the way Nesteros treats "what is declared by the very words." For him, understanding the literal sense of scripture does imply that we believe and seek to act on what the words say. In other words, it is knowledge that we receive and not merely understanding.

Furthermore, Nesteros's interpretation was shared by the prominent theologians of the early church. For example, in Basil's sermons on the opening chapter of Genesis, the *Hexaemeron*, he explicitly sets aside the allegorical meaning of the text and seeks to treat only the literal. Even though the words of Genesis can be understood to some extent by anyone, believer or unbeliever, Basil is constantly pointing out their real significance for the life of believers: God did in fact create the universe, and the universe reveals God's power, wisdom, and goodness—just as the words say. Believers are thus to look at nature and to praise God for what they see, and to conduct their lives in accordance with God's commandments. Although the literal sense differs from the other three senses of scripture, for Basil it still gives spiritual, or theoretical, knowledge.

For Nesteros there is the literal and historical sense of scripture and there are the three "spiritual" senses. Today we tend to use the word "spiritual" in opposition to "material," but that is not how it is used by Nesteros. Among the earliest Christians, "spiritual" refers to what is proclaimed in the Bible—the meaning of the words themselves. Sometimes even the letters making up the words have theological or spiritual significance. Nonetheless, the term "spiritual knowledge" is also used in a narrower sense to refer to three particular kinds of meaning found in the scriptures: the allegorical (or typological); the moral (or tropological); and the mystical (or anagogical) senses of scripture.

Nesteros explains the meaning of all four senses of scripture by referring to chapter 4 of Paul's letter to the Galatians, where the apostle develops an allegory linking Hagar and Sarah, Ishmael and Isaac, Sinai and Jerusalem, and the old and new covenants. The historical sense concerns the past—what is recorded as having happened. Paul's statement in verses 22-23 is an example of this:

> For it is written that Abraham had two sons, one by a slave woman and the other by a free woman. One, the child of the slave, was born according to the flesh; the other, the child of the free woman, was born through the promise.

The historical sense concerns only what is apparent, visible on the surface, but it points us toward the allegorical, toward what is hidden and not yet revealed. Thus Paul, continuing his argument, writes,

> Now this is an allegory: these two women are two covenants. One woman, in fact, is Hagar, from Mount Sinai, bearing children for slavery. Now Hagar is Mount Sinai in Arabia and corresponds to the present Jerusalem, for she is in slavery with her children. (Gal. 4:24-25)

Through allegory, an event that happened in the past can be understood in a new way at a later time. In this case it is the establishment of the covenant at Sinai by Moses and the event which Sinai prefigures: the new covenant established by Christ. Before the coming of Christ, the covenant with Moses was a mystery, not fully comprehensible; afterward, it can be understood as an anticipation of what is to come.

It is, Nesteros notes, "the moral explanation that has to do with the improvement of life and practical teaching, as if we were to understand by these two covenants practical and theoretical instruction." The moral sense has two aspects— practical and theoretical. What Nesteros calls "practical" we might call "spiritual"; he means that something of the spiritual sense is available to unbelievers, just as some understanding of the active life of repentance, control of the passions, and love of neighbor can also be understood by anyone. But not *all* its meaning can be grasped by unbelievers, since the moral sense also has a contemplative aspect, which Nesteros calls "theoretical." Contemplative knowledge is possible only for believers. That is why characterizing the tropological sense as simply the moral significance of any text does not bring out this and other subtleties in the exegesis of ancient teachers.

The highest sense, according to Nesteros, is the anagogical, or mystical sense of scripture, as Paul further explains in Galatians:

> But the other woman [Sarah] corresponds to the Jerusalem above; she is free, and she is our mother. For it is written, "Rejoice, you childless one, you who bear no children...for the children of the desolate woman are more numerous than the children of the one who is married." (Gal. 4:26-27)

The "Jerusalem above" exists in the present as the mother of Christians. It is a present reality affecting us now. The anagogical sense is more sublime because it conveys our ultimate destiny, the consummation of God's promises, and so is associated with the eschatological sense of scripture.

After this extended series of examples, Nesteros shows how the four senses of scripture may converge on a single theme:

> One and the same Jerusalem can be taken in four senses: historically, as the city of the Jews; allegorically, as the Church of Christ; anagogically, as the heavenly city of God "which is the mother of us all"; tropologically, as the soul of man, which is frequently subject to praise or blame from the Lord under this title.

Nesteros makes it clear that spiritual knowledge, which includes all four senses of scripture, is not available to everyone. It requires an effort to overcome evil passions and behavior, a commitment to follow Christ, and a desire for God's presence. This requirement is understood when he speaks of the four senses of scripture in the context of the spiritual journey: "In vain then does one strive for the vision of God, who does not shun the stains of sin."

The spiritual knowledge conveyed by allegory is not available to anyone without the coming of Christ. Nesteros takes for his example Paul's text from 1 Corinthians:

> Our ancestors were all under the cloud, and all passed through the sea, and all were baptized into Moses in the cloud and in the sea, and all ate the same spiritual food, and all drank the same spiritual drink. For they drank from the spiritual rock that followed them, and the rock was Christ. (1 Cor. 10:1-4)

He then explains that only with the coming of Christ is it possible to know that the ancient Jews passing through the Red Sea were baptized. Only with Christ's coming is what was hidden made manifest. So too, the manna from heaven and the water from the rock that Moses struck prefigure the body and blood of Christ given to us in the eucharist. These revelations, which are the heart of the allegorical reading of scripture, are by their very nature is hidden until Christ comes. Those who receive Christ as God's work are able to understand events such as the Exodus as both the salvation of the ancient Jews from bondage in Egypt and an intimation of the salvation from sin and death wrought by Christ. Unbelievers may find this a more or less plausible interpretation, but they do not receive any knowledge of God.

What is true of the allegorical sense is true of the mystical sense. It concerns the future when Christ returns in glory; accordingly, it is focused on Christian hope, the life of the world to come, and the eschatological meaning of a text. All Christians are even now receiving from God the life that is to come, and so the anagogical sense of scripture is frequently used to guide them on their spiritual journey. For example, the frequent use of the Song of Songs as a symbol of Christ's love for his church, or for the individual believer, is an anagogical reading.

⌣   ⌣

These ancient methods of interpreting scripture in the light of the spiritual journey have been set aside by modern biblical scholarship. Yet questions that we regard today as part of modern biblical criticism, such as textual issues, were also vigorously pursued in their day by theologians, such as Origen. Moreover, Erasmus and other Renaissance scholars revived this tradition, while Martin Luther was greatly interested in the relationship of the Epistle of James to the letters of Paul. So critical study was practiced well before the modern period, but much of this traditional interpretation did not help with the critical problems raised by history. For example, traditionally Moses was said to be the author of the Pentateuch because of such New Testament passages as Mark 7:10, in which Jesus tells the Pharisees and scribes, "For Moses said, 'Honor your father and your mother.'..." If Mark's gospel claims that Moses spoke these words, then to deny Mosaic authorship of the first five books of the Bible was considered an attack on the truth of the New Testament.

The first step of modern critical studies was to insist that matters such as authorship and historical sequence had to be established independently of the New Testament. Accordingly, more and more emphasis was placed on an historical interpretation of the text—that is, understanding the text in terms of the intentions and circumstances of the writer. This was a very valuable development. For example, it enabled us to see that prophets were not attempting to predict the future, but to speak God's word to people of their time, which indeed had a future dimension insofar as their message concerned the fulfillment of God's promises. In time, the Old Testament was seen by scholars primarily as the historical background for the New Testament, with intrinsic religious value. But it had ceased to be interpreted spiritually—that is, not as the term "spiritual" was understood in the fourfold senses of scripture, with allegorical and anagogical significance.

This neglect has a downside for present-day biblical scholarship that is not immediately apparent because modern critics often fail to make the important distinction between allegory and typology. Allegory, in which the literal text ("what is declared by the very words") is used to yield hidden meanings, may at times be exaggerated and excessive. A good example is Augustine's interpretation of the parable of the Good Samaritan, in which "the traveler stands for Adam, Jerusalem for the heavenly city from which he fell, Jericho for his resulting mortality, the thieves for the devil and his angels, the wretched plight in which they left him for the condition to which he was reduced by sin, the priest and the Levite for the ineffective ministrations of the old covenant, the Samaritan for Christ, the inn for the Church," and so on.[2]

Excessive or not, typology strives to show the unity of the Old and New Testaments by discovering points of correspondence between the Hebrew and Christian scriptures. Typology interprets some event or person in the Old Testament as a type or a foreshadowing of Christ, or some other event or person in the New Testament. We saw an example of typology in Nesteros's reference to I Corinthians 10:1-11, where Paul treats the events of the crossing of the Red Sea, the giving of manna in the wilderness, and the water struck from a rock as corresponding to Christian baptism, holy communion, and Christ. Unlike allegory, which is often said to provide no check to subjective fantasy, typology is guided by the kind of correspondences the New Testament itself specifies.[3] Typology in the New Testament rests on the theological conviction that Jesus is the Messiah, the one who had been promised to Israel.

The writers of the New Testament use Old Testament correspondences to interpret or state who Jesus is and the significance of what he does, but they do not present this practice as their invention. According to the New Testament, Jesus himself established a correspondence between the Jewish Passover and his coming death, when at the Passover meal he presented himself as the Lamb to be sacrificed for our salvation. As one scholar writes,

What justifies understanding the Bible typologically (if it can be justified) is the conviction that God is always the same. If he is fully known in Jesus Christ, then when he revealed himself under the old dispensation, he must in some sense have been known as the God of Jesus Christ. It is, therefore, justifiable to seek in his revelation of himself under the old dispensation some similarity with his revelation under the new. In fact, a sort of typology can be found in the Hebrew Bible itself: see, for example, Isaiah 43:1-19; 51:9-11, where God's action of old in creation and redemption from Egypt are treated as types of the new deliverance from exile about to occur.[4]

Additionally, the Old Testament may also have a meaning beyond that recognized by its authors, and with the coming of Christ this deeper sense can be perceived by the writers of the New Testament and by Christians today. For example, Psalm 23 can be read by a Christian, who knows Christ as the Good Shepherd, as applying to Jesus, while realizing that this is not what the psalmist had in mind. But to do this in a way that is not forced requires strong similarities between the text and Jesus—as is the case in this instance between God as shepherd and Jesus as shepherd.

According to the scholar Leonhard Goppelt in his book on typology, the New Testament authors handle the significance of historical events and teaching by presenting Jesus as the fulfillment in history of God's promises to the people of the Old Testament.[5] For example, Matthew shows the correspondence between Jesus and the Jewish people: Jesus, after his baptism, is tempted in the wilderness for forty days and nights, as the Jews, after they were baptized by passing through the Red Sea, were tempted in the wilderness for forty years. In his temptations in the wilderness, Jesus is triumphant, showing his power to resist the temptations of Satan, in contrast to the people of Israel, who succumbed in the wilderness trial. Jesus is Israel—Israel as it ought to be, fully obedient. Similarly, Matthew's gospel sees a correspondence between Jesus and Moses: Jesus delivered a set of teachings from a "mount" (the Sermon on the Mount) just as Moses gave the people of Israel the law which he had received on Mount Sinai. Here too Jesus is greater, for at his baptism Jesus received the Holy Spirit and was declared God's Son.

Typology is often criticized for its treatment of history: the meaning the New Testament writers find in past events is not the meaning the writers of the Old Testament had intended. But this criticism fails to see that the very essence of typology is its conviction that what was in the older events is only brought to light *when Jesus Christ becomes known.* Such a reading of the Old Testament assumes that throughout biblical history God has been acting for human redemption, showing only in part what was to come in Christ. It assumes a divine sovereignty over history, so that people, events, and writings have a significance beyond what they were thought to have at earlier times. As the philosopher Charles Taylor puts it,

> The sacrifice of Isaac was seen as a type of the sacrifice of Christ. In this outlook, two events are linked through something outside history, when their symbolic affinity reflects some deeper identity in regard to Divine Providence....In spite of the immense temporal gap, there is a sense in which they are simultaneous.[6]

This view runs counter to the belief that the history of ancient Israel consists of events that can be confirmed or vindicated apart from the convictions about Jesus held by the New Testament writers. To modern biblical students who seek above all to understand texts in terms of the historical circumstances of the people who wrote and read them, typology and Christian doctrine are a positive hindrance. But the only way to exclude typology as legitimate is on theological grounds: that is, only if Jesus is not the fulfillment of the Old Testament promises, as New Testament writers and theologians claim.

If the typological thinking of the New Testament writers is ignored, then a biblical scholar has neglected a part of the task of critical history. Typology is essential to understanding what the New Testament says to be true about Jesus. Even if an individual scholar personally rejects (for example) the correspondence between Jesus and the people of Israel, or Jesus and Moses, as an historian he or she cannot deny that the writer of Matthew understood the significance of Jesus in those terms. Likewise, an individual scholar personally may not accept the correspondence between the Last Supper and the Jewish Passover, but a biblical scholar, as an historian, cannot rightly ignore that this is how several New Testament writers expressed and understood the death of Jesus. Therefore, the ancient and medieval church's spiritual understanding of the Bible *to the extent* that it is typological and not allegorical remains valid for those who receive Christ as the fulfillment of God's promises to Israel.

The New Testament's treatment of biblical figures as models for the spiritual journey is also of continuing value. As we saw in our discussion of ascetical theology, growth in virtue is the first division of the threefold way and part of the spiritual journey. It is not only necessary for enhancing the ability to love our neighbor as ourselves, but it is also a necessary condition for achieving purity of heart, the primary motivation for the contemplative life. So the moral sense of scripture applies both to the active life and the contemplative life.

Here biblical people are identified as exemplars of particular virtues, as in Gregory of Nyssa's *Life of Moses*: "Scripture teaches us that Noah was righteous, Abraham faithful, Moses meek, Daniel wise, Joseph chaste, Job blameless, and David greatsouled."[7] This practice of using biblical figures as moral and spiritual models, however, relates to a common criticism of typology today. A typological reading of scripture is frequently said to undermine the Hebrew scriptures and the religion of ancient Israel, in effect reducing the Old Testament to a mere prefiguration of the New. But a typological reading is not to be taken in isolation. The same people who read the Bible typologically (or for that matter, allegorically) read it in the moral and anagogical senses as well.

✌ ❀

The anagogical sense of scripture is concerned with the full establishment of God's kingdom when Christ returns in glory. By derivation, the anagogical sense was applied to the spiritual journey of individuals into God. Moses in particular was not only an exemplar of the virtue of meekness or humility (the moral sense of scripture) and a type prefiguring Jesus (the typological sense), but his entire life was considered to be a model of the spiritual journey into the contemplative life for Christians to imitate. To read scripture for guidance on the spiritual journey into contemplation is to read it anagogically.

For Gregory of Nyssa, Moses was the preeminent example of a spiritual person. The alternative title to Gregory's book *Life of Moses* is *Concerning Perfection in Virtue*, and he uses Moses as the basis for giving the reader "some counsel concerning the perfect life."[8] Moses is a guide for the spiritual journey because he went as far into the contemplative life as it is possible to go. Gregory points out that God appeared to Moses in a burning bush, giving him an illumination that we too can receive if we follow his path:

> It is upon us who continue in this quiet and peaceful course of life that the truth will shine, illuminating the eyes of our soul with its own rays. This truth, which was then manifested by the ineffable and mysterious illumination which came to Moses, is God.[9]

God also appeared to Moses in the darkness of Mount Sinai, which Gregory understood to mean Moses was directly before God, without any mediation, such as the burning bush provided:

> What does it mean that Moses entered the darkness and then saw God in it? Scripture teaches by this that religious knowledge comes at first to those who receive it as light.[10]

Gregory understood the Christian life as neverending growth in virtue, because in the spiritual life we live more and more in God. Since God is unbounded, we never cease growing in knowledge and love. This is evident in the life of Moses. Because Moses knew God in the light of the burning bush and in the darkness of the cloud, he desired to know God not only according to his present human capacity, but fully. God granted Moses' desire. God placed Moses in the cleft of a rock and passed before Moses. Moses saw the back of God. This is because God is unbounded; to know God is ever to be following behind God.

Thus Moses, even though he lived before Christ, is portrayed as having achieved what all Christians aspire to achieve: a life that forever increases in virtue through following God. Moses shows what perfection is: neverending growth in knowledge and love because one is forever following God into the unbounded life of God. The theological conviction that lies behind the ancient and medieval church's use of scripture in spiritual formation, liturgy, doctrine, morals, and art is found in Paul's rich statement,

> For it is the God who said, "Let light shine out of darkness," who has shone in our hearts to give the light of the knowledge of the glory of God in the face of Jesus Christ. (2 Cor. 4:6)

The Word of God spoken at creation is the source and organizing principle of the cosmos. The same Word that was spoken by God at creation shines in our hearts so that we may have knowledge of God by looking to Jesus Christ. Scripture is the witness or testimony to that Word in creation, in our hearts, and in Jesus Christ.

Notes

1. For Nesteros and the fourfold interpretation of scripture, see John Cassian, *Conferences*, in *Nicene and Post-Nicene Fathers*, 2nd series, Philip Schaff and Henry Wace, eds. (Grand Rapids: Eerdmans, 1955), 11: 435ff.

2. See J. N. D. Kelly, *Early Christian Doctrines* (New York: Harper, 1958), 70.

3. For an important recent defense of allegorical thinking against this common charge, see David Dawson, *Allegorical Readers and Cultural Revision in Ancient Alexandria* (Berkeley: University of California Press, 1992). See also Leonhard Goppelt, *Typos*, D. G. Madvid, trans. (Grand Rapids: Eerdmans, 1982).

4. A. T. Hanson, "Typology," in Metzger and Coogan, eds., *The Oxford Companion to the Bible* (New York and Oxford: Oxford University Press, 1993), 784.

5. Goppelt, *Typos*.

6. Charles Taylor, *Sources of the Self* (Cambridge, Mass.: Harvard University Press, 1989), 288.

7. Gregory of Nyssa, *The Life of Moses*, Everett Ferguson, trans. (New York: Paulist Press, 1978), 20.

8. *Ibid.*, 29.

9. *Ibid.*, 59.

10. *Ibid.*, 94.

CHAPTER TEN

MYSTICAL THEOLOGY

When we meditate on the natural world, we come to see the glory of God through its order, harmony, and beauty. As the Bible and Christian theology clearly teach, however, even then we are not able to grasp God's nature or essence. Through God's workings in nature and self-revelation through scripture, we are able to learn a great deal about God; even so, God remains hidden. We cannot imagine, nor can our minds grasp, God's unbounded fullness. So when we say that the glory of God is revealed through the books of nature and scripture, we are simultaneously aware of God's hiddenness. We must consider this idea of the hiddenness of God more fully before we can examine the third division of the threefold way, which is the direct knowledge of God face-to-face.

God's glory and God hiddenness are two aspects of God that are simultaneously present. Let us try to say this another way, using the alphabet and the musical scale. The letters that go to make up any word are separated from each other by blank spaces, while musical notes are separated from each other by silences. By perceiving the letters and the notes, and the pattern of blank spaces between them, we can read the words on the page and hear the sounds of the musical notes. God's activity and God's hiddenness are similar. God is at the same time known—like the letters of the alphabet and the notes of the score—and not fully comprehensible—like the blank spaces and silences. This is true not only of the manifestation of God's glory in nature, but also of his revelation in scripture and in prayer. This is why Christian theology teaches that God remains hidden, as the prophet Isaiah so graphically put it, "Truly, you are a God who hides himself" (45:15).

In theology this idea of the hiddenness of God is often described by making use of the classic distinction between *cataphatic* and *apophatic*. The cataphatic way (the "way of affirmation" or *via positiva*) is balanced by the apophatic way (the "way of negation" or *via negativa*). The *via positiva* affirms that God, as the source of the universe, possesses all the qualities of creatures in the highest degree. We cannot, however, form a proper conception of those qualities as they are found in God, because God as creator is in a different category from creatures. We can say, for example, that God's knowledge is infinite or without limit, but we cannot fully conceive of this. We can understand that God knows all that can be known, but God, unlike us, does not rely on evidence or reasoned arguments to gain knowledge. God does not arrive at knowledge. God just knows. That is all we can say.

What is true of knowledge is true of all the properties of God. What we can conceive of God's properties, or "perfections" as they have traditionally been called in Christian theology, is so inadequate that we must balance all our affirmations with a qualification. That is the *via negativa*, the apophatic way: we have to say that the words or qualities adequate to describe creatures do not fully describe God, the creator. In order to speak with greater accuracy, we therefore have to negate or reject our affirmations because God surpasses anything that we can say about him. God can be known, but all our ideas fail to comprehend God and none is fully adequate. We can also say that God is unknowable, but with the qualification that we are able to say things that are true of God, such as, "God knows all that there is to be known."

Dionysius the Areopagite is the main source of the way of negation in Christian spirituality, especially through his book *Mystical Theology*. But the truth that lies behind the way of negation appears throughout the Bible. We see it in the absence of any representation of God in the Holy of Holies of the Temple, indicating the essential hiddenness or holiness of God. Following the way of negation is motivated by the desire to avoid idolatry: worshiping what is less than God. Whenever we think that we are able fully to grasp and understand God just as we can grasp and understand any other created thing, we are prone to idolatry.

Dionysius went so far as to claim that *everything* we say of God must be balanced with a negative in order to avoid idolatry. If we say God is creator, for example, we must also say that we cannot imagine or conceive God's creative activity because God does not create as we do. All human creativity is at best only a faint analogy to God's. Similarly, all causal relations—impact, generation, electronic impulses—express in various ways the dependence of one thing upon another and so tell us something about the dependence of the universe on God. But all of these are inadequate; they can only begin to suggest *how* the universe is dependent on God. With the instruments of science we can detect and measure the impact of one force upon another, or the speed of an electronic impulse, but we cannot detect or measure God's creative activity in establishing and sustaining all the parts of the universe—including those phenomena we are able to measure. God's creativity is boundless, without limit, and takes place at every moment. Even though we know the universe is not self-explanatory, but instead is dependent on God, we still cannot conceive of God's activity in creating and sustaining the universe.

While asserting that God is creator, therefore, at the same moment we have to deny every idea of creativity and causality learned from the study of our own creativity and from the principles of cause-and-effect operating in the world about us. This does not mean that we are denying God's creativity, but affirming that this creativity is not like our own, nor is it like the creative powers of nature. Instead, we are affirming the super-abundance of God.

In this way, the nature of God's creativity is hidden from our minds. We also need to understand that our ignorance is appropriate: we know what we do not understand and why we do not understand it. Only when this is the case is the idea of mystery accurately used in theology. To invoke mystery in any other circumstance is a mistake, or, even worse, a cover for laxity of thought.

To put it somewhat differently, the cataphatic way indicates a *quantitative* difference between God and God's creatures: to say God is all-powerful means that God is more powerful than anything else. By contrast, apophatic statements indicate the *qualitative* difference: not only is God more powerful than anything else, God's power is also the source of all power. The positive and the negative go together, like letters in a word and the blank spaces between them, or like the notes that make up musical sounds and the silence between the notes. Together they represent two aspects of the same reality; neither can stand apart from the other. Every positive statement about God has within itself an implicit negation, and every negative statement an implicit affirmation. To say that God is creator means both that God's creative activity is greater than the creativity of his creatures *and* that we cannot conceive of it in the first place. To perceive God's glory through the order, harmony, and beauty of the universe is to recognize at the same time that the universe does not contain God.

⌣ ∾

In I Corinthians St. Paul teaches us that we will all know God "face-to-face" after death (13:12). But from the time of the early church onward it was also believed that for some Christians, face-to-face encounter with God is possible in this life, especially because of Paul's claim that he himself once experienced being "caught up to the third heaven" (2 Cor. 12:2). Some Christians have the urgent desire to know God's presence not only through nature and scripture, but directly, without any intermediary. They seek to be "nakedly" present to God; that is, without anything between them and God, including any thoughts and images.

The late fourteenth-century English mystical treatise *The Cloud of Unknowing* is an excellent example of the spiritual ascent that culminates in meeting God face-to-face. It is by an unknown writer who translated Dionysius the Areopagite's *Mystical Theology* into Middle English. The author of the *Cloud* had a powerful yearning for the direct presence of God; he suffered the deep anguish and frustration of a lover who is separated from the beloved. It is the same ardor that Paul expressed when he said that for him to die was gain because then he would reach the goal of life, to be fully with God in Christ. Encountering God's presence through nature, human nature, and the words of scripture was not enough to satisfy such a yearning—only a direct encounter with God would suffice. The author stresses, however, that the desire to be fully with God is not felt, nor meant to be felt, by everyone. So the book was written primarily for those who have this vocation, although he hopes that other Christians might profit by it as well.

Its author is well acquainted not only with the writings of Dionysius, but also with the theology of Thomas Aquinas. Thomas taught that through analogies we can make true statements about God, and gain an opaque but nonetheless genuine knowledge of God. Although Thomas's doctrine of analogy is a less misleading way to treat the hiddenness of God than that of Dionysius, it too did not yield a sufficient knowledge of God to satisfy this theologian who longed to be with God utterly face-to-face, in this life. Because he had learned from both Dionysius and Thomas that the human mind has only limited and indirect access to God through concepts and images, he turned from the use of the mind to rely solely on love.

The author of *The Cloud of Unknowing* also claimed to have discovered a way to encounter God through a distinctive kind of prayer. Even though the mind cannot fully conceive of God, and so come to God through the intellect, it is possible to reach God by "a naked love." By abandoning all thoughts and images we enter into darkness, as Moses did when he entered the dark cloud on Mount Sinai. If we enter this darkness with a pure or naked love, utterly focused on God and God alone, God meets us in a "cloud of darkness." Because we have dropped all thoughts and images, God is directly and fully present to us through love. We now "know" God, not with our mind, but with pure love. It is from this meeting of God in darkness, not with the intellect but with love, that the book derives its title. It is through our *unknowing* (emptying our minds of all thoughts and images) that through love we know God.

The reason we are to set aside all thoughts and images is that, however sound they may be, they are not able to grasp God's essence. For the author of the *Cloud*, practice of the way of negation is done in prayer. In prayer we are to forget all that we know, to empty the mind utterly, and to be left only with a naked love for God—"naked" because all thoughts and images have been abandoned.

This can be misleading, however. It may appear to us that to empty the mind of all thoughts and images is to set aside the positive way—that is, to avoid saying anything whatever about God. Actually what we are to do is to concentrate our attention on the blank spaces between the letters, on the silences between the musical notes of music. These empty spaces and these silences only exist because of the letters and notes. With ardent love we attend to the hiddenness of God, and to the darkness that surrounds all God's acts as creator and redeemer.

This mystical theologian assumes that the reader of his treatise has already achieved considerable mastery over the passions and is well advanced in the love of neighbor and of God. His treatment also assumes that as we practice the prayer that helps us to enter the darkness, we will continue to attend regular worship services, probably several times a day, and to read and pray the scriptures. *Lectio divina* is recommended for both beginners and proficients. He recommends that we alternate between regular worship activity and the prayer that leads into the darkness—between discursive meditation and prayer, and imageless and wordless prayer. For although the prayer that enables one to enter the darkness is simple to state, it is very difficult to achieve. It is one thing to say we are to empty our minds of all thoughts and images, but it is another thing to do it.

The theologian Austin Farrer has a wonderful analogy to explain the relationship between regular but ordinary spiritual activity and the "prayer of forgetfulness," as it is sometimes called. Farrer compares our coming to know and love God to the stages of ordinary human friendship. At first, he writes, there was

> a time of intense mental activity when we were comparing the actions and opinions, the habits and expressions of our friend, and trying to make them fit. We thought we knew the person more vividly than we had ever known any one, and then found ourselves suddenly baffled; a stranger stood before us, and we began all over again. There was such a time, but it came to an end at last, and we knew our friend, not as God knows his creature, but as well as one creature hopes to know another. To bring our friend before us we no longer needed to make explorations in the field of memory. We had only to say the name "John" or "Mary," or whatever it might be....
>
> There was a time when the lover of God, like the lover of Mary or John, was putting together his knowledge of God, gathered piecemeal from reflection on the ways and works of God, as they are delineated in the creed and recognized in life. But again, there was a time, not so soon reached but reached at last, when the knowledge of God gathered round the Name of God; and though it remained often profitable to explore one by one his glorious works, and necessary often to wrestle in particular with the interpretation of his ways, yet it was good, and indeed best of all, to be quiet at the place from which sprang all the paths of light and name the Name of God, giving up the soul entirely to that unity of all perfection for which the Name had come to stand.[1]

For the same reason, the author of the *Cloud* recommends that someone who is trying to pray use a single word, such as "God," "fire" (an allusion to the Holy Spirit), or even a plea like "help" for entering the darkness of unknowing. It is discursive prayer that is being set aside, not who and what God is. All that we have learned of God is made present to us in a single word. If we are called to know God face-to-face and, in humility, continue to practice the prayer of forgetfulness, in time one enters the cloud of darkness. It is pure love for God responding to God's love that draws us in.

I want to emphasize that however different God is from all creatures, the love of God that is God and that can be experienced in this life is God without qualification. Because we can all experience the love of God in this life, the divine love that is God does give us knowledge of God. Divine love is the one positive affirmation that does not need to be balanced with a negation. Such love is experienced before entering the cloud of unknowing, since it is divine love that motivates us to seek it. Divine love is also experienced by those who are never called to seek a face-to-face encounter with God. However different the life to come may be from this life, one thing we experience in this world will be present in the world to come—and that is God's love. As Paul said in 1 Corinthians 13:8, "Love never ends."

We must also emphasize a striking difference in spiritual theology concerning knowledge of God face-to-face. Even though the author of the *Cloud* is influenced by Dionysius, following the way of negation in prayer in order to gain access to God, he describes meeting God face-to-face in terms of *habitual* presence—not, as in Dionysius, an ecstatic moment. For Dionysius the moment of meeting God face-to-face is rare, fleeting, and ecstatic. In that moment all distinctions between subject and object disappear, and we lose all consciousness of our surroundings; we are unable to hear other people speaking, and can temporarily lose control of our body. This experience is similar to what are commonly called mystical or ecstatic states. In this aspect, Dionysius has influenced a major stream of Christian spirituality, including Latin Christianity. But the *Cloud* author explicitly states that the encounter with God in love is not ecstasy, but another kind of presence:

> On the other hand there are some who by grace are so sensitive spiritually and so at home with God in his grace of

contemplation that they may have it when they like and under normal spiritual working conditions, whether they are sitting, walking, standing, kneeling. And at these times they are in full control of their faculties, both physical and spiritual, and can use them if they wish, admittedly not without some difficulty, yet without great difficulty. We have an example of the first kind [a state of ecstasy] in Moses, and of the second in Aaron....

Moses could only "see" on rare occasions, and then after much hard work, but Aaron on the other hand, by virtue of his office, had it in his power to see God in the temple behind the veil as often as he liked to go in. Aaron symbolizes all those I have mentioned who by their spiritual wisdom and assisted by grace may achieve perfect contemplation whenever they like.[2]

Here rare moments of ecstasy are contrasted to what is traditionally called habitual presence: prayer under "normal working conditions." It is made very clear that meeting God directly in love is not the rare or momentary ecstatic state that Dionysius describes as union with God. For the *Cloud* author, meeting with God face-to-face is possible as frequently as the contemplative, by God's grace, attends to God. Moreover, he calls this knowledge of God in love "perfect contemplation," indicating that habitual presence is indeed union with God.

This means that we should not identify the third part of the threefold way, union with God, with states of ecstasy, as is so frequently done. The author of the *Cloud* goes so far as to claim that habitual presence is superior to rare, ecstatic moments:

Those who achieve [union with God] at first but seldom, and only with great effort, shall afterwards have it when they will and as often as they like. Moses again is our example, who at first could only see the ark in a sort of way, rarely and after great effort on the mountain, but afterwards, as often as he liked, saw it in the valley.[3]

We may perhaps go even further and say that the habitual presence of God described here can be known through the practice of *lectio divina*, or spiritual reading. This kind of meditation is clearly a different route, but the habitual presence of God mediated by *lectio* and the direct knowledge of God through face-to-face encounter are essentially the same. In each case, it is the same love of God that is known and that will be known in all eternity. In addition, the love that motivates the ordinary Christian in prayer and holy reading need be no less pure than the love that motivates the rare contemplative who seeks a "naked" love. As Austin Farrer said of friendship, there are some for whom attentiveness to God is still a matter of painstakingly recalling, one by one, the ways and works of God, while for others God springs to mind in all fullness through a single word. This interpretation helps to lessen the disparity between the indirect and direct love of God; it is not a matter of kind, but simply of degree.

⌣: ~

The goal of the Christian life—both in this world and the world to come—is union with God. But this union should not be identified with ecstatic states, even though such states occur. More fundamental to union with God is our sense of God's continual presence, an inner stillness that is available to all Christians. This habitual presence is to be in constant prayer, to be always present to God and to know that God is always present to us.

Support for this view comes not only from the tradition of the western church, from which *The Cloud of Unknowing* derives, but also from the eastern church in the practice of the Jesus prayer. This prayer is familiar to many people because of the spiritual classic written by an anonymous Russian layman of the nineteenth century entitled *The Way of the Pilgrim*, although the prayer itself is at least as old as the fourth century. It takes the form of a simple repetition: "Lord Jesus Christ, Son of God, have mercy on me" is the most common form. Sometimes the words "have mercy on me, *a sinner*" are added. Other variations include "have mercy on *us*," rather than "on me." The prayer is repeated again and again in a rhythmic fashion. It is not a mantra—a phrase repeated over and over in order to achieve a suspension of all thought—but an *address* to Jesus Christ, with the explicit affirmation that this Jesus is the incarnate Son of God. The prayer is to lead us into the divine presence, just as the very short prayers do that are recommended in *The Cloud of Unknowing:* "God" or "fire" or "help."

The Jesus prayer is simply another way to lead us from discursive thought and prayer ("indirect" knowledge of God) to nondiscursive thought and prayer—"direct" knowledge of God, or silent contemplation (in Greek, *hesychia*). Of this union with God, the contemporary eastern theologian Nicolas Cabasilas writes:

> Everyone may continue to exercise their art or profession. The general may continue to command, the farmer to till the soil, the workman to pursue his craft. No one need desist from his usual employment. It is not necessary to retire into the desert, or to eat unaccustomed food, or to dress differently, or to ruin one's health, or to do anything reckless; for it is quite possible to practice continual meditation in one's own home without giving up any of one's possessions.[4]

The only significant difference between the author of *The Cloud of Unknowing* and those who teach silent contemplation in the eastern church is that, for the author of the *Cloud*, union with God is only for the few who have the vocation to seek God face-to-face. In the eastern church, as we have just seen, union with God is the vocation of every Christian, regardless of occupation.

Notes

1. Austin Farrer, *Lord I Believe: Suggestions for Turning the Creed into Prayer* (Cambridge, Mass.: Cowley Publications, 1989), 11-12.

2. *The Cloud of Unknowing and Other Works*, Clifton Wolters, trans. (New York: Penguin Books, 1987), 146-147.

3. *Ibid.*, 148.

4. As quoted by Kallistos Ware in "Ways of Prayer and Contemplation," in *Christian Spirituality: Origins to the Twelfth Century*, Bernard McGinn and John Meyendorff, eds. (New York: Crossroad, 1985), 412.

CHAPTER ELEVEN

CHRISTIAN DOCTRINE AND THE SPIRITUAL LIFE

Throughout this book I have talked about Christian spirituality as the attempt to shape our lives in accord with Christian doctrines, and to have lives that match the truth they enshrine. I have concentrated on showing how Christians today can explore and use the spiritual disciplines and practices of the past, with a focus on the age-old image of the threefold way and the contemplation of God through nature and scripture.

In closing I want to raise one more question that has come up several times already, and that is the noticeable gap today between theology as it is taught in the academy and the practice of Christian devotion. It is typical of academic theology today to focus chiefly on questions that are extrinsic rather than intrinsic to theology. Intrinsic questions arise from the nature of God and of ourselves in relation to God. Extrinsic questions arise from somewhere else: what we have learned, or think we have learned, from fields of inquiry other than religion. For example, if we hold a view of scientific laws that seems to imply that miracles are impossible, or a theory of culture that seems to imply that Christian belief is no more than the product of cultural forces, the questions these theories cause us to raise are all *extrinsic* to theology. In terms of sheer quantity, probably most of a theologian's work today will be directed toward extrinsic questions, since there are so many new intellectual, technical, and cultural developments that need to be understood in the light of God. But if theologians do not work through the intrinsic questions first, they miss out on the spiritual formation that can arise from this struggle. This neglect greatly contributes to the gap between intellectual inquiry and the devotional life.

Questions about the nature of God's reality and our human capacity to know God are intrinsic to theology. God's essence far surpasses the power of our senses and intellect to know it, and that explains the absence of any representation of God in the Holy of Holies in the Temple of ancient Israel. It also underlies Thomas Aquinas's claim that God is not a member of any genus, and neo-orthodoxy's emphasis that God is not a being among beings, but wholly Other. God can only be revealed by God. God has done so in many ways: to the people of ancient Israel through the prophets and to Christians in Jesus Christ.

Because human sinfulness has clouded our hearts and minds, receiving God's revelation requires repentance; an increase in our understanding of God's revelation requires continuing spiritual growth. That is why intellectual inquiry cannot be *detached* inquiry, and why Julian of Norwich compared the knowledge of God to three wounds: the wound of contrition (repentance and continuing repentance for one's disobedience); the wound of compassion (love of neighbor); and the wound of longing (love for God). People can be taught theology and, given intelligence and diligence, perform well as theologians, but this may be no more than a knowledge *about* God. Richard of St. Victor stresses that it is useless for us to know about God unless we have a longing for God, because

it is vain that we grow in riches of divine knowledge unless by them the fire of love is increased in us. For love arising from knowledge and knowledge coming from love must always grow in us, each ministering to the increase of the other by mutual growth, and love and knowledge developing in turn.[1]

Both Julian's and Richard's understanding of the Christian life is centered on becoming more like God. An increase in our understanding of God leads in turn to an increase in our love for God and our love for neighbor, and in our neighbor's love for us. This understanding is common to all Christian spirituality. A divorce between intellectual inquiry and spiritual formation occurs when intellectual inquiry is not concerned with movement toward God, and it happens quite easily because spiritual growth is not a prerequisite for discussing doctrines. Doctrines themselves do not include our response, whereas our response is the focus of devotion.

The crucial question is, how may we find God and remain in the presence of God, who is beyond the capacity of our senses and intellect? As we have said, it is only by God's self-revelation. But in order for us to know God we must also respond by receiving God's self-revelation and so begin our journey into God. Our lives must increasingly be formed by God. There is no detached knowing of God—any more than there is a detached love of neighbor or a detached attitude toward sin and failure. The intellectual inquiry that is intrinsic to theology requires personal involvement and an aspiration to know and love God; it is inquiry that forms us spiritually.

For most of Christian history, intellectual inquiry and spiritual aspiration toward God has gone hand-in-hand. In his treatise *Proslogion* St. Anselm begins, as he always does when he engages in intellectual inquiry, with meditations to awaken the mind from its torpor.

> Come now, little man,
>   turn aside for a while from your daily employment,
>   escape for a moment from the tumult of your thoughts.
> Put aside your weighty cares,
>   let your burdensome distractions wait,
>   free yourself awhile for God
>   and rest awhile in him.

Enter the inner chamber of your soul,
  shut out everything except God
  and that which can help you in seeking him,
  and when you have shut the door, seek him.
Now, my whole heart, say to God,
  "I seek your face,
  Lord, it is your face I seek."[2]

Anselm believes that in order to increase our knowledge of God through intellectual inquiry we must always begin by seeking to free ourselves from all distractions so that we may desire God with our whole heart. Rather than having our minds and hearts filled with a multitude of desires pulling us in different directions, we must focus on God, whom we hope to come to know face-to-face by increasing our understanding of God.

This heartfelt meditation occurs *before* Anselm presents his ontological proof. In this reflection on God's existence, Anselm comes to understand that God's existence is not like the existence of everything else that exists or might exist. God's existence is a *necessary* existence. Through his intellectual search, Anselm has come to understand something he had not understood before, but had believed and loved. He has found a precise way to distinguish between God and the world, thereby preventing the mind from confusing God with what is not God—an idea that proved very useful to Bonaventure. With this understanding, he has now drawn closer to God whom he has been seeking.

Anselm is convinced that theological inquiry is possible only for someone who has been converted to a spiritual perspective. His inquiry, like that of his master, Augustine, is based on belief. Anselm writes, "I do not seek to understand so that I may believe, but I believe so that I may understand; and what is more, I believe that unless I do believe I shall not understand."[3] He does not think he has to solve all sorts of problems extrinsic to theology, rising from other types of inquiry, before he can believe. And he does not think that unless he does so, he cannot engage in theological inquiry. As a practicing Christian Anselm is already engaged with the reality of God; because of that engagement, he believes and loves, seeking further understanding in order to know and love God better.

Not all types of spiritual formation are concerned with intellectual inquiry. For example, Bernard of Clairvaux focuses much of his attention on the earthly life of Jesus, especially on his crucifixion, and is emotionally affected by gazing on them lovingly in prayer and meditation. By virtue of an increasingly purified love, he hopes to achieve a closer and closer unity with God. Bernard is not concerned with intellectual inquiry, as were the academic theologians of the universities. He is quite content with the doctrinal orthodoxy he inherited.

Ignatius Loyola owed a great deal to the affective spirituality of St. Bernard, and in his *Spiritual Exercises* he relies heavily on the use of the imagination. We are to bring before our mind's eye various events of the life of Jesus as vividly as possible, so that we may be affected by them. As we increasingly commit ourselves to Christ's kingdom, we are to seek to discern God's intention that we might do God's will. Thus Loyola's use of contemplation differs from the contemplation in speculative spirituality. There contemplation is to increase our understanding and love of God until it culminates in knowledge of God face-to-face. Loyola's spirituality is explicitly a *practical* spirituality. Contemplation is used to form oneself spiritually so that one is better able to discern and to do God's will in daily life.

Nor is all speculative spirituality concerned with intellectual inquiry. For example, Evagrius of Pontus, so important for the ascetical theology of the eastern church and, through John Cassian, a major influence in the West, focused almost exclusively on pure prayer as the means to knowledge of created beings and of God face-to-face. Continuing intellectual inquiry into the meaning of Christian doctrines, either by him or by others, seems to have no role in his understanding of our spiritual ascent.

There are, however, some types of speculative spirituality in which intellectual inquiry is integral to the spirituality. We can see this clearly in Bonaventure's writings. In *Disputed Questions* on the Mystery of the Trinity, Bonaventure is inquiring into the divine life of the Trinity: the movement within the inner life of God as Father, Son, and Holy Spirit. Then he uses what he has learned from this intellectual inquiry in his spiritual classic, The Soul's Journey into God. What he has learned from his study forms the rungs of a ladder, so to speak, for the ascent into the life of God. Bonaventure's inquiry into the movement in the inner life of God is guided by what God has revealed God to be, Father, Son, and Holy Spirit. God's own self-revelation is Bonaventure's starting point for seeking to understand the movement in God's divine life. Goodness is by its very nature self-communicative, and God is the highest good. God gives wholly, as fully as possible. The Son is uniquely related to the Father, existing with the Father and the Holy Spirit in an eternal movement of giving and receiving that is so full and complete that Father, Son, and Holy Spirit are one God, one divine life.

Bonaventure makes the Trinity accessible to thought and thus to contemplation. In the first six parts of The Soul's Journey into God, it is what can be put before the mind for contemplation that is vital for the soul's ascent. In the prologue he stresses—as do Julian, Richard, and Anselm—that we need to be involved with God in order to know God. Although Bonaventure is writing for believing and practicing Christians, he emphasizes that his readers must prepare themselves with an earnest intention of ascending into the life of God. Otherwise, as he emphasizes in his prologue, the knowledge he imparts will be useless.

Inquiry into the Trinity, so often an occasion for baffle-ment—even embarrassment— for many Christians, becomes in Bonaventure's hands part of our spiritual journey. He tells us what to think about as we contemplate the movement in God's inner life as Father, Son, and Spirit, and how, by thinking about them, to move more fully into the life of God. Bonaventure's intellectual work on the Trinity, presented in meditative form, immensely heightens our understanding of God's transcen-dence and generosity. Contemplating the movement in God's life, which Bonaventure has made accessible to our under-standing, ignites an intense desire for God. Our love for God may be so purified and heightened that we may, even in this life, experience in a moment of ecstasy the presence of God face-to-face. At first sight intellectual inquiry into the movement in God's life may seem a most unpromising place to look for anything significant for our spiritual formation, but in *The Soul's Journey into God* Bonaventure shows it is just the opposite.

Simone Weil once said that we can compare the task of theology to that of a flashlight: it casts light that enables us to see. In theology we seek to see all things in the light of God, but if we do not wrestle with the questions that arise out of God's very nature, then our batteries will be weak and the bulb will cast insufficient light. A theologian's vocation is to understand the self-revelation of God so that it casts light on all areas of thought and life, including those matters that challenge the vocation itself.

❧ ❧

Throughout this book my concern with yesterday's spirituality has been above all to find what is useful for today. I have not hesitated to indicate what I myself find useful, but I have not intended to be prescriptive. My focus on *Christian* spirituality throughout this book, moreover, does not imply that other great religions of the world fail to yield substantial spiritual help. It is much more profitable for Christians, however, to study the spirituality of other faiths and compare them to Christian spirituality after they have learned what Christian spirituality itself is. As we have seen, to gain a significant knowledge of Christian spirituality and actually to practice it is itself a very demanding task, and that is why this book examines only Christian spirituality.

Furthermore, there is a very large amount of spirituality today that makes little or no reference to Christian doctrine whatsoever. Joseph Campbell, who became a major spokesman on spirituality with his books on mythology, told Bill Moyers in a television interview that he did not need faith or doctrines of any sort at all because he had experience. He did not mean experience *of* anything in particular; by experience Campbell meant feelings. As long as we experience feelings of exhilaration, consolation, or comfort, then the question of what reality is and the task of living in accordance with it need not arise. One of the attractions of New Age spirituality is its vagueness about what is true outside one's own self.

I remember introducing a series of talks in a local church by saying that Christian doctrine was important not because it was helpful but because it was true. The congregation was dumb-founded. How could any well-educated person today equate religion and truth? Like so many people who attend church, they found theology abstract and boring; they disliked dogmatism and doctrinal wrangling. Too much Christian teaching, they said, demands that we believe something and too many teachers of Christianity try to impose these beliefs on people, violating their integrity in the process. This congregation, like so many others, was very understandably not interested in doctrinal teachings.

To look only for what is *helpful* in Christianity, largely because of this uneasiness at affirming its doctrines, has become a common practice both inside and outside the church. One of the reasons that the study of religion is popular today in universities and colleges is that students can be exposed to religious ideas and, by a kind of spiritual osmosis, hope to be uplifted; they do not want to face questions about the truth of religious claims or submit to spiritual discipline. But there is a price to be paid. If we are concerned with finding help only, and not with truth, we are unlikely to find substantial help. For when we actually come face-to-face with temptation, danger, and death, we encounter reality—and at that point the question of who or what will guide and sustain us is no longer a side-issue. It cannot be put off indefinitely, pending further scholarly research. This is probably why "spirituality" in general, in spite of its initial appeal, fails us. When the chips are down, vagueness about what we believe is not an asset.

Christian doctrine is not a strait-jacket, nor are we to submit to it mindlessly. Rather, Christian doctrine guides us through the maze of life. "Doctrine" means "teaching," and "dogma" means "authorized teaching." In Christian spirituality, you are asked to learn what Christianity teaches, and its dogmas are those teachings which, after long and continuing examination and controversy, specify what is judged to be authentically Christian. Christian doctrine does not have to be taught "dogmatically," that is, pushed onto us in an authoritative way. Christian teachers are susceptible to this vice, but those who object are often themselves dogmatic in insisting that we should be vague. The answer is not to turn toward vagueness, and thereby lose the concreteness of Christian teachings.

If we neglect Christian teaching, we will miss a great deal. People who try to understand and live in accordance with Christian teachings often find that their entire outlook changes. Both their hearts (what they treasure) and their minds (what they find important) are transformed as they rise to a new awareness of themselves, the world, and God. But if we treat Christian teachings casually and only concern ourselves with spirituality, those things that Christian doctrines enable us to perceive about ourselves, our world, and God are likely to remain hidden. We remain enclosed within our limited perspective, unable to understand even the most elementary Christian teaching. As Ludwig Wittgenstein, considered by many to be perhaps the greatest philosopher in the twentieth century, said:

> In religion every level of devoutness must have its appropriate form of expression, which makes no sense at a lower level. This doctrine, which means something at a higher level, is null and void for someone who is still at the lower level; he can only understand it *wrongly* and so these words are not valid for such a person.[4]

If we are not serious about trying to shaping our life in accordance with Christian teachings, however tentatively we first hold them to be true, then the substantial help we need is unlikely to be available to us and our understanding will remain inadequate. To ask that Christian doctrines be taken seriously by those who are concerned with spirituality is not a baseless demand for conformity, but an invitation into contact with God, who will help us and lead us to greater knowledge.

Notes

1. Richard of St. Victor, *Selections from Contemplation*, Clare Kirchberger, trans. (London: Faber & Faber, 1957), 161.

2. *The Prayers and Meditations of Saint Anselm with Proslogion*, Benedicta Ward, trans. (Harmondsworth, England: Penguin, 1973), 239.

3. *Ibid.*, 344.

4. Ludwig Wittgenstein, *Culture and Value*, Peter Winch, trans. (Oxford: Basil Blackwell, 1980), 32e.

Index

Cowley Publications is a ministry of the Society of St. John the Evangelist, a religious community for men in the Episcopal Church. Emerging from the Society's tradition of prayer, theological reflection, and diversity of mission, the press is centered in the rich heritage of the Anglican Communion.

Cowley Publications seeks to provide books, audio cassettes, and other resources for the ongoing theological exploration and spiritual development of the Episcopal Church and others in the body of Christ. To this end, it is dedicated to developing a new generation of theological writers, encouraging them to produce timely, creative, and stimulating publications of excellence, and making these publications available widely, reaching both clergy and lay persons.